BITTER HARVEST

BITTER HARVEST

AN ANTHOLOGY OF
CONTEMPORARY IRISH VERSE

Selected and Introduced by

JOHN MONTAGUE

CHARLES SCRIBNER'S SONS
New York

Charles Scribner's Sons
Macmillan Publishing Company
866 Third Avenue, New York, NY 10022
Collier Macmillan Canada, Inc.

Permissions acknowledgments appear on page 211

Library of Congress Cataloging-in-Publication Data
Bitter harvest: an anthology of contemporary Irish verse/ selected
and introduced by John Montague.
p.   cm.
Includes indexes.
ISBN 0-684-19032-X
1. English poetry—Irish authors.   2. English poetry—20th
century.   3. Irish poetry—Translations into English.   4. English
poetry—Translations from Irish.   5. Ireland—Poetry.   I. Montague,
John.
PR8858.B5   1989
821'.914'0808916—dc19   88-19026
                                                      CIP

Macmillan books are available at special discounts for bulk purchases
for sales promotions, premiums, fund-raising, or educational use.
For details, contact:

Special Sales Director
Macmillan Publishing Company
866 Third Avenue
New York, NY 10022

10 9 8 7 6 5 4 3 2 1
Printed in the United States of America

In memory of poet Austin Clarke,
and publisher extraordinaire *Liam Miller of the Dolmen Press*

Contents

xi

xii

Against the Grain

This anthology is both a supplement to my previous, a survey of Irish verse from the earliest times; and a statement, amounting to a proud claim. As the earlier anthology showed, Irish poetry has a long tradition, from probably the oldest vernacular in Western Europe to what is called, for convenience' sake, the Irish Literary Renaissance, when Irish writers in English won a worldwide reputation. Yeats, Joyce, Shaw, Synge, and O'Casey are household names, a rich tapestry of masters, representing perhaps the only real victory to which we should aspire.

This tradition of independence is continued by Samuel Beckett, but it is not sufficiently understood that his generation was a remarkably rich one. The coincidence in time of Patrick Kavanagh (1904–1967), Padraic Fallon (1905–1974), Brian Coffey (b. 1905), Louis MacNeice (1907–1963), John Hewitt (1907–1987), Denis Devlin (1908–1959), and the senior poet in Irish, Maírtín Ó Direain (1910–1988) suggests a powerful interplay of forces which would make a proper anthology of the period a salutary revelation of how talent will survive, against the grain of a hostile climate.

The relationship between literature and the immediate form of history we call politics is both subtle and brutal. It seems no accident that the earlier burst of great writing coincided with a redefinition of Ireland, leading to the creation of binary political entities, contrary allegiances. The North and South of Ireland, to deploy the usual shorthand, involved the establishment of two separate parliaments within a year of each other, and the fostering of two—one overt, the other covert—basically sectarian states.

Now that uneasy stalemate is being challenged by bomb, bullet, and some hopeful argument. Whatever the outcome, and there may well be none for some time, our withers are being wrung. For it is against this hectic backdrop that these poets strive; they are neighbors of nastiness, contemplatives of chaos. This obviously applies to those of Ulster background but, with the increasing illiberalism, agitation, and recession in the Republic, disaffection is general. The land is tense with a menaced mildness, as Paul Muldoon's "Ireland" shows:

> The Volkswagen parked in the gap,
> But gently ticking over.
> You wonder if it's lovers
> And not men hurrying back
> Across two fields and a river.

Because of such pressures, some of the best poetry in the English-speaking world has been written in Ireland since the Sixties. And now with younger writers like Michael Davitt and Nuala Ní Dhomhnaill, as well as the bilingual Hartnett, Irish holds equal sway. I see four generations, hard at work. My own has been elevated into a relatively senior position, because of the deaths of many of our elders, the gifted generation described above. But we were always trailed by a wilder ragtag and bob-tail of intellectual nomads like O'Grady and Simmons, a half-way house before the task force of Northern poets arrived, following my own pioneer trail. The publicity given—and often sought by—the Ulster poets obscured their Southern contemporaries, although happily, young writers from the Republic are writing back, especially in Irish. The issues are less topical, but the pens are as sharp in Cork as Belfast, from Galvin to Tom Mc Carthy.

So you have the compelling phenomenon of two diseased bodies politic infecting each other with antiquated maladies, while the poets chant remedies. There is a sense in which Ireland has become a field of irreconcilable forces, from the craven refusal of the South to countenance abortion and divorce as necessary evils, to the religious racism of the North; it is hard to feel proud of either place. Kinsella's self-inflicted journey into the self, the corpse count in Heaney, Longley, and Muldoon, suggest the atmosphere, swathes of darkness, as in my own

Dead Kingdom (1984). But our deepest yearnings lie elsewhere; Longley's "Peace" and Heaney's "Harvest Bow" are charms for our heartsick land, and a different emphasis would have produced a crop of love poems. Derek Mahon is an increasingly marvelous poet, with a millennial vision. The grotesqueries of Muldoon find a feminine counterpart in the extravagance of Nuala Ní Dhomhnaill's Irish, which recalls a time when Irishwomen were more than equal. This exfoliating achievement in two languages, at least two traditions, works to redeem the systematic degradation of the whole island. As Kinsella prescribes for the poetic enterprise:

> cut as it were, in the sinews
> of our souls; each other's worst company;
> it is we, letting things *be*,
> who might come at understanding.
> That is the source of our patience.

I have cast my net wide, to indicate the fury of activity, but no anthology could keep up. Despite the recession there is a more vibrant literary scene than when Kinsella and I set out. Now a young writer has a choice of publishers: Gallery, Blackstaff, Raven Arts, Dedalus, and others, and there is a healthy crop of literary magazines and prizes. Remembering the hungry Fifties, I contemplate it all with cheerful envy. How far we are from Austin Clarke publishing his own later work, from a house that is now disappeared, and Liam Miller's lonely pioneering efforts with the Dolmen Press, which is also gone. To their tenacity in bad times I dedicate this bitter, but provident, harvest.

Whence turbulent Italy should draw
Delight in Art whose end is peace....

—W. B. YEATS

BITTER HARVEST

Francis Stuart

b. 1902

REMEMBERING YEATS

Shadow on shadow his mind
Raised a temple of thought
And his aging body, blind,
Groped to the inner court
To hide itself from death,

We sat with our guests after the meal
As they talked of Yeats and sipped their wine
And I wondered would they never go
As under the table I felt your heel
While they spoke high art and quoted a line
From the Purgatorio.
Who was it had known all Dante once?
And why—though why not—had he called me a dunce?

He was rather rhetorical
And chose the wrong buddies.
In his august presence my blood ran cool
And my mouth dried up,
But he had his passion
As have only the great ones.
Yeats, we drink to you
In your final solitude.

Brian Coffey

b. 1905

from THE DEATH OF HEKTOR

Homer   where born where buried of whom the son
what journeys undertaken known not   His work
abides witness to unfaltering sad gaze constrained
A harp he uses   background for verses sung
He pared no fingernails not indifferent   not masked
Light we suppose once had entered eyes to brand memory
with noon's exact flame of sun mirrored in wind-stirred sea
Black night for death   Colours of morning evening for life
the rose the glaucous the amethystine wave-work carpeting
maimed anatomy black white red of man at war
screams the women keening patience the emptied hearts
His ears open to spoken word and words down time like
      wind-blown sand
words of triumph unsleeping enmities wound-up spells
      malice
swirl of sound continual mixed in a perfect ear
surfacing coherent truer than history all and everything

Prudent Homer who survived to make his poems
did he keep unsaid wordly in innermost anguished heart
what would not have pleased his client banqueters
nor reached by resonance the hearts of self-approving lords
yet at last might reach our raddled selves

from ADVENT

III

what have they done to Klio what have they done to our
      Muse

2

of History Muse Klio of Memory daughter and set
out of place and time on a plinth to reign of silence queen

As if in opened bunker one faced numberless suppliant bones
and awed by that silent thunder wanted words

What would we call on you for Klio if your style
were finger on lip to crawl through cunning corridors
fumbling behind the arras for what was not there

Is it really Klio who silent endures the flogging of ass-hide
when beat of soldierly song pleasures the newly great

How bear to watch her impassive face at noon
when waft of distant carnage spices graeco-roman smells

Klio would you have me accept your state of bondage
at a slick rhymester's hands   Oh help me proclaim
under full moon of harvest heaven lovely of face and sought
by lovers planting two by two memorials of joy
you Muse present and veiled whenever murder is out

No trouble to watch ruin-builders at work "No loss of nerve"
"No going back" they bay "Prophets of doom to the wall" So'll
Bullfrog say as Bullfrog is "Expand Bigger Better Expand"
"Only" says Bullfrog so mincingly croaky "Only
growth counts" while grinding salt-mills grind on
Sea the saltier taste the bitterer and white verges spread
"Grind on grind on" Bullfrog roars glutted know-all

And that's picking vibes up from the surround
No need to judge No charge to lay of hybris
In that yarn Bullfrog professionally deformed
must subside to a soft machine

Now far from respect and reverence what we have seen
we tell   Look   Eagle pinned to topmost big-top

3

cleared path to the beak no Hooplas tumbling quipping
to flatter drooping purpose fill vacancies with self-conceit
Here dragons here powers malign   Watch
stern abstracted Crier precede Chief tighten tension
with drum-beat sole-slap heel-click halt

See who now comes surging out of that silence
Kilroy really here master to mastered come to rule

Still he faces them moans *They sigh* seeks a beat and finds
"What have they done to you my people what have they done
        now"
They groan he works and twists *They scream* mute he
drops hand openly weeps lowly resumes

"I never asked for shame to crawl through loyal hearts
I never wanted drawn-sword blood-spill wrath and pain"

"For us I wanted warm seas clear light dreams unfurled
I wanted for you world unending and in your tears
to hold you to my heart my people trust for trust"

"You my people who alone feel shame of loss
who now intend our journey back to the sun
faith where to find for sure not in father mother
sibling friend or love-in-bed where but in me"

"Far from plain of grass stiff in ice-wind searching
far from ribbed sand and spinifex our cornfield space"

"Fail we in weather's worst we shall hang in siren-web
our want our right maybe but still the wind
to blow hairs two by two from our heads blow them away"
"Remember we shall birth-right and knife-in-back
Come what may triumph we shall or else drag all down
Thus my people thus shall we"   *cocorico cockadoodledoo*
and ere he swags with mighty lung blares "YES"

4

So spun so coiled his reasons round them
fed them spell of *Selves Alone*
No sun sets on us   This world our home
Our country right or wrong   and correctly
led them through crashing gods into eyeless night

All over now   purple gold gun drum stench of victory
far as eye-scan where sunflower had followed white sun
white crosses north south east west recede into patient moss

Childsong birdsong force maimed men women forlorn
to suppose nations may recover from war
Sharp Seeclear wooers of Klio's praise
now scrabbles through zones of Memo Mountain for proof
paper like punter pinning hope to saddle like rune reader
does surface to shout if p then q easing no decent doubt
no whirlwind quizzer'll ever void his desk

As if *als ob* one could say what's next in line
In line what a gas when it moves what an it
by surge and leap retreat enclosure decoy deceit
in depth by broad sweep from nail clipping to holocaust

"O little ship ahoy" hopeless hand from ocean hails

Deed after deed age after age like fashion a trace of seen
      before
suppliants at altar-horn the beaten across table-top beg time
pity with justice in short supply lied to later slain
curse of the goddess dormant in chancellery quiet as cancer
peredyshka it dazzles our eyes Klio in mirror play instance
Plataea men slain women slaves   ad infin victims dooms

Klio silent confers no laurel crown best that way since muse
like spirit single is and soul of work's diversity
in poem quickening clear view of what we are

allowing tale-teller chance of prudence after event
invites to silence when best is guess

Silence its quality is not famed as mercy is
flowers like Cassandra an absence present
foresight may fail hindsight feed fool now is the dark
where in quiet may sound breathing and beating heart

Years late not one sure hour in hand one asks
who are these easy figures grouped under spring sun
by thousands grasshopper clasp of gold in hair linen white
painted shrines garish behind half-circle ranks
smoky kitchen twittering wife out of mind on day of purging
Viewing place with priest's throne face skene dancing floor
readied for poet to reconcile unknown god with men

It starts   House of Atreus black hole in light
incest rape murder obscenity
knotted vipers poison like damp on walls
a reek of malice
Watchman to warn of victory's deceiving fire
Ancients flickering from hope to despair
still or weaving in febrile dance
The god's decree   Wisdom is won through woe
Queen impeccable a norm
Herald to kiss Argive earth announce the King

Weak as Adam Agamemnon tramples the blood-red rug
enters home to be killed
"neither clothed nor unclothed
nor in water nor on dry land
nor in palace nor outside
snared apple at lips in net"
in ritual vestige of early lost ways
So gleams the curse in new death
murder new with special touch

wife kills husband her ravisher
fingers her son to murder her
and who will work curse on son
at crossways where rival furies rend

So was myth worked to poet's will
to teach viewers how god heals
by old evil out and clearly veiled the awesome dark
will favour city of reason and care
while viewers take new hearts home

For one day on that open floor
Athens was cosmos god and kings and men
not even slave who shares with freeman but death
forgotten nor women mystery stars
quite unlike those tumblers circled by close crowd
whose threadbare mat's patch of green
seemed "lost in the cosmos forlorn"
like a band-aid on soiled hand

Poet then displayed to wakening eyes
the drama   what now goes on
and humbled men maybe began to be wise

But history corn with tares
lumpers and issue of soup
casual shrug of quaking earth
spider lair of queen den of monster king
toil with desert toil with fertile field
building demolishing daily ups and downs
surface mere product of uncounted aims
births marriages and deaths so it moves

The veil of randomness attracts lawseeking yen
constants to find to make necessity of
while history works still against the rounded tale

"Over the hill enemy mine does prosper overmuch"
envy one of history's oldest friends
till compromise partition induce civil war

Sincerity now questioned motive assailed blood spilled
habit's thinking forced to confusion in prevailing deceit
trust dead one kills lest one be killed
the most honest come to rage and rend
from both outside and within evil no vested interest
fouls and slimes and spreads with savage rule
till history's mercy is oblivion start elsewhere
history earth's unfinished business
who could tell the story to its end
when no necessary thought will usher in final night

from ADVENT

VII

"My son my son" the Blakean figure mourns and affirms
"You did not see your grievings etched already in me
not hero nor arrant coward human only everyday"

What they had done had been done again by him
until youth's grand display induced forgiveness
while on ahead it still surged supposing admiring crowd
joy to share with H for Hero outdated classic style

Mothers know of us all from memorable point of growth
One such will say of her early-dead "He was strange
from start went in his dream leading not led
choosing and doing outside of rules in deathwards race"

The early-dead do not it seems want niche of glory
refuse reign for an hour as if possessed seem heroes

recover daily heart and sense in sure final grasp
recall for us Cuchulain turning with perfect manners from
     fight
when battle glory its fierce light faded in torn frame
bound himself to upright stone so fairly to greet
equal foe man to man and gently decline to earth

But behind untimeliness in tossed pretence of real order
design mere sketch act half-willed blurred effect
veiled by record petrified in grey stone

What lies ahead "somewhere somewhen" soon enough for
     one and all
rage curiosity fear distaste anguish parting like living various
Best like Denis* to go hoping to meet a pleasant Lord

Our memories get filled with names like vases piled in half-
     light
and shifting shades sadness a hope and regret in silent rooms
all this side what clear to eye and ear heart and final touch

He had pictured his bad day unnumbered times
had assumed the mood and habit of early death
cleanly then had noted his broken limbs
told nurse where he hurted and at close of smiles and doing
sanguine alone had turned off what he had become from world
     and us

At term free and in dark faith one can take stand
in act of vanishment like most far and swiftest star
to where eye cannot enter whence no sound returns not a
     silence
                                             nothingness
more vehement than our whole knowing how it was here

*Denis Devlin, diplomat and poet, d. 1959.

9

Living he wore a cross laid to earth his body bears that cross
sign of intention love of death abandonment to last surrender
in downfall collapse to bits and pieces seeming failure
giving what he was without mask to a father unseen

corse   rule
           aspen
           silver
lead   salt
spell   glass

owl   glow
black   hag

seal   yew

John Hewitt

1907–1987

ULSTER NAMES

I take my stand by the Ulster names,
each clean hard name like a weathered stone;
Tyrella, Rostrevor, are flickering flames:
the names I mean are the Moy, Malone,
Strabane, Slieve Gullion and Portglenone.

Even suppose that each name were freed
from legend's ivy and history's moss,
there'd be music still in, say, Carrick-a-rede,
though men forget it's the rock across
the track of the salmon from Islay and Ross.

The names of a land show the heart of the race;
they move on the tongue like the lilt of a song.
You say the name and I see the place
Drumbo, Dungannon, or Annalong.
Barony, townland, we cannot go wrong.

You say Armagh, and I see the hill
with the two tall spires or the square low tower;
the faith of Patrick is with us still;
his blessing falls in a moonlit hour,
when the apple orchards are all in flower.

You whisper Derry. Beyond the walls
and the crashing boom and the coiling smoke,
I follow that freedom which beckons and calls
to Colmcille, tall in his grove of oak,
raising his voice for the rhyming folk.

County by county you number them over;
Tyrone, Fermanagh . . . I stand by a lake,
and the bubbling curlew, the whistling plover
call over the whins in the chill daybreak
as the hills and the waters the first light take.

Let Down be famous for care-tilled earth,
for the little green hills and the harsh grey peaks,
the rocky bed of the Lagan's birth,
the white farm fat in the August weeks.
There's one more county my pride still seeks.

You give it the name and my quick thoughts run
through the narrow towns with their wheels of trade,
to Glenballyemon, Glenaan, Glendun,
from Trostan down to the braes of Layde,
for there is the place where the pact was made.

But you have as good a right as I
to praise the place where your face is known,
for over us all is the selfsame sky;
the limestone's locked in the strength of the bone,
and who shall mock at the steadfast stone?

So it's Ballinamallard, it's Crossmaglen,
it's Aughnacloy, it's Donaghadee,
it's Magherafelt breeds the best of men,
I'll not deny it. But look for me
on the moss between Orra and Slievenanee.

POSTSCRIPT, 1984

Those verses surfaced thirty years ago
when time seemed edging to a better time,
most public voices tamed, those loud untamed

as seasonal as tawdry pantomime,
and over my companionable land
placenames still lilted like a childhood rime.

The years deceived; our unforgiving hearts,
by myth and old antipathies betrayed,
flared into sudden acts of violence
in daily shocking bulletins relayed,
and through our dark dream-clotted consciousness
hosted like banners in some black parade.

Now with compulsive resonance they toll;
Banbridge, Ballykelly, Darkley, Crossmaglen,
summoning pity, anger and despair,
by grief of kin, by hate of murderous men
till the whole tarnished map is stained and torn,
not to be read as pastoral again.

TRYST

Coming up the green lane from the sea,
that bramble-trellised unfrequented lane,
on a hot summer Sunday afternoon
we suddenly glimpsed a couple to our surprise,
a handsome tall young priest and a young nun
standing face-to-face, oblivious
of all around: the priest's blond head was bowed,
the nun's face uplifted; a romantic tryst,
life aping art, minor Preraphaelite—
Halliday or Hughes? Most likely Arthur Hughes—
the sunlight flashing through the dappled leaves,
the convent's roof-tiles bright above the trees,
across the broad field at the lane's last gate.
Confer a title, explicate the theme:
illicit love at risk, a perilous moment

which mocked the vows; two hearts in jeopardy,
or simply Brother and Sister briefly held
in family bondage with some hint of treason.
Averting gaze in hushed embarrassment,
we hurried past, unanswered, deeply moved.

Maírtín Ó Direain

1910–1988

BERKELEY

On a rock, Bishop of Cloyne,
I was reared as a boy;
And the grey stones
And barren crags encompassed me,
But far from such you lived,
Bishop and philosopher.

Swift himself, the great Dean,
Was not mad, if it's true
He left you on his doorstep;
Was not the closed door a dream
In your mind, for thus you taught?
And why would he want to open it for you
Since it was only a ghost of itself?

Dr. Johnson too
Kicked an adjacent stone
As if the assault
On the pure entity smashed
Your vision, and its implication
That in the mind was contained
All living substance and all inanimate matter.

I don't deny I agreed
With those great men for a while,
But since the grey stones began
To turn to dreams in my mind,
I do not know, my dear Bishop,
That you weren't the one who went on the deep
While the great men stayed on the shore.

THAT FACE

Take care of that face!
It is not fully yours
But you have it on loan
From the staunch women of our race.

When I stretch my memory
I see it on a hundred women—
The women of our people who were sent
Beyond Galway to the West.

Women who learned forbearance
During the long slow wait
For the pitiable reward—
They left their mark on that face.

There is another mark on that face—
Of women who hid their pride
The time they got the alms
That left a chink in their honour.

The speakers of Irish are scattered
Around the surface of the globe
Without government or state,
Without a leader among them.

Take care of that face!
It is not fully yours
But you have it on loan
From the staunch women of our race.

AXLE SONG

Where have you been this long time.
Song of the axle?
Hidden in time's backyard
Though many a night long ago
You were music to my ears.

Andy Goill's cart behind a good horse
Was climbing the slope
On the way to Ownaght.
My mind's eye tells me
It was painted bright red,
But that's not my keenest memory
Nor what I miss the most,
But the song of the axle
That lulled me to sleep.

THE ESSENCE IS NOT IN THE LIVING

When fire and drink were a shelter
From the blast of the cold night
You were a compact bundle of sensuousness—
The warmth of the fire before you,
The cheering wine at your side;
But you were still intent on your interests
In spite of fire, drink and warmth,
But you were not the essence of an island
Nor any of the group who were with you.

The old lord on the wall
With his formal paunch,
And his good lady facing him
With her formal bust,
Have been captured in two portraits

Unliving and unchanged
For three hundred years and more—
Those two are the essence of an island,
As are stone rock and strand
In the cold midnight.

Unliving things slip
Away from life and leave it:
Was it thus
The island left my poem,
Or did you notice?

Translated by Douglas Sealy
and Tomás MacSiomóin

Patrick Galvin

b. 1927

MY FATHER SPOKE WITH SWANS
for Gráinne Maria

Leaning
On the parapet
Of the South Gate Bridge
My father spoke with swans
Remembering his days
With the Royal Munster Fusiliers.

India was dawn
The women cool
The sun cradled in my arms.
Sometimes
When the clouds were wine
I washed my face in the Ganges.

The swans rose from the Lee
And held their wings.

2

Leaning
On the mysteries
In her twilight room
My mother spoke with God
Remembering Pearse
And the breath of Connolly.

Ireland was green
The men tall
The land mirrored their brightness.
Sometimes

When the eagles call
I walk the roads to Bethlehem.

God opened his eyes
A loss for miracles.

3

From these two
I was born
The Ganges swaying with the Lee
And gunfire rising to a fall.
My mother wore black till she died
My father died with swans.

Only the rivers remain
Slow bleeding.

PLAISIR D'AMOUR

SPRING

My father
Against the victories of age
Would not concede defeat
He dyed his hair
And when my mother called
He said he wasn't there.

My mother, too
Fought back against the years
But in her Sunday prayers
Apologised to God.
My father said there was no God
"And that one knows it to her painted toes."

My mother smiled.
She'd plucked her eyebrows too
And wore a see-through skirt
With matching vest.
"He likes French knickers best" she said
"I'll have them blest."

My father raged.
He liked his women young, he said
And not half-dead.
He bought a second-hand guitar he couldn't play
And sang the only song he knew—
Plaisir d'Amour.

SUMMER

When summer came
My father left the house
He tied a ribbon in his hair
And wore a Kaftan dress.
My mother watched him walking down the street
"He'll break his neck in that," she said—
"As if I care."

He toured the world
And met a guru in Tibet.
"I've slept with women too" he wrote
"And they not half my age."
My mother threw his letter in the fire—
"The lying ghett—he couldn't climb the stairs
With all his years."

She burned her bra
And wrote with lipstick on a card—
"I've got two sailors in the house
From Martinique.
They've got your children's eyes."

My father didn't wait to answer that
He came back home.

And sitting by the fire
He said he'd lied
He'd never slept with anyone but her.
My mother said she'd never lied herself—
She'd thrown the sailors out an hour before he came.
My father's heart would never be the same—
Plaisir d'Amour.

AUTUMN

Through autumn days
My father felt the leaves
Burning in the corners of his mind.

My mother, who was younger by a year,
Looked young and fair.
The sailors from the port of Martinique
Had kissed her cheek.

He searched the house
And hidden in a trunk beneath the bed
My father found his second-hand guitar.
He found her see-through skirt
With matching vest.
"You wore French knickers once" he said
"I liked them best."

"I gave them all away," my mother cried
"To sailors and to captains of the sea.
I'm not half-dead
I'm fit for any bed—including yours."
She wore a sailor's cap
And danced around the room
While father strummed his second-hand guitar.

22

He made the bed
He wore his Kaftan dress
A ribbon in his hair.
"I'll play it one more time," he said
"And you can sing."
She sang the only song they knew—
Plaisir d'Amour.

WINTER

At sixty-four
My mother died
At sixty-five
My father.

Comment from a neighbour
Who was there:
"They'd pass for twenty."
Plaisir d'Amour.

THE MADWOMAN OF CORK

To-day
Is the feast day of Saint Anne
Pray for me
I am the madwoman of Cork.

Yesterday
In Castle Street
I saw two goblins at my feet
I saw a horse without a head
Carrying the dead
To the graveyard
Near Turner's Cross.

I am the madwoman of Cork
No one talks to me.

When I walk in the rain
The children throw stones at me
Old men persecute me
And women close their doors.
When I die
Believe me
They'll set me on fire.

I am the madwoman of Cork
I have no sense.

Sometimes
With an eagle in my brain
I can see a train
Crashing at the station.
If I told people that
They'd choke me—
Then where would I be?

I am the madwoman of Cork
The people hate me.

When Canon Murphy died
I wept on his grave
That was twenty-five years ago.
When I saw him just now
In Dunbar Street
He had clay in his teeth
He blest me.

I am the madwoman of Cork
The clergy pity me.

I see death
In the branches of a tree
Birth in the feathers of a bird.
To see a child with one eye
Or a woman buried in ice
Is the worst thing
And cannot be imagined.

I am the madwoman of Cork
My mind fills me.

I should like to be young
To dress up in silk
And have nine children.
I'd like to have red lips
But I'm eighty years old
I have nothing
But a small house with no windows.

I am the madwoman of Cork
Go away from me.

And if I die now
Don't touch me.
I want to sail in a long boat
From here to Roche's Point
And there I will anoint the sea
With oil of alabaster.

I am the madwoman of Cork
And to-day is the feast day of
Saint Anne.
Feed me.

Richard Murphy

b. 1927

SEALS AT HIGH ISLAND

The calamity of seals begins with jaws.
Born in caverns that reverberate
With endless malice of the sea's tongue
Clacking on shingle, they learn to bark back
In fear and sadness and celebration.
The ocean's mouth opens forty feet wide
And closes on a morsel of their rock.

Swayed by the thrust and backfall of the tide,
A dappled grey bull and a brindled cow
Copulate in the green water of a cove.
I watch from a cliff-top, trying not to move.
Sometimes they sink and merge into black shoals;
Then rise for air, his muzzle on her neck,
Their winged feet intertwined as a fishtail.

She opens her fierce mouth like a scarlet flower
Full of white seeds; she holds it open long
At the sunburst in the music of their loving;
And cries a little. But I must remember
How far their feelings are from mine marooned.
If there are tears at this holy ceremony
Theirs are caused by brine and mine by breeze.

When the great bull withdraws his rod, it glows
Like a carnelian candle set in jade.
The cow ripples ashore to feed her calf;
While an old rival, eyeing the deed with hate,
Swims to attack the tired triumphant god.
They rear their heads above the boiling surf,
Their terrible jaws open, jetting blood.

At nightfall they haul out, and mourn the drowned,
Playing to the sea sadly their last quartet,
An improvised requiem that ravishes
Reason, while ripping scale up like a net:
Brings pity trembling down the rocky spine
Of headlands, till the bitter ocean's tongue
Swells in their cove, and smothers their sweet song.

A NEST IN A WALL

Smoky as peat your lank hair on my pillow
Burns like a tinker's fire in a mossy ditch.
Before I suffocate, let me slowly suck
From your mouth a tincture of mountain ash,
A red infusion of summer going to seed.
Ivy clumps loosen the stonework of my heart.
Come like a wood pigeon gliding there to roost!

I float a moment on a gust sighing for ever
Gently over your face where two swans swim.
Let me kiss your eyes in the slate-blue calm
Before their Connemara clouds return.
A spancelled goat bleats in our pleasure ground.
A whippet snarls on its chain. The fire dies out.
Litter of rags and bottles in the normal rain.

Your country and mine, love, can it still exist?
The unsignposted hawthorn lane of your body
Leads to my lichenous walls and gutted house.
Your kind of beauty earth has almost lost.
Although we have no home in the time that's come,
Coming together we live in our own time.
Make your nest of moss like a wren in my skull.

MORNING CALL

Up from the trawlers in the fishdock they walk to my house
On high-soled clogs, stepping like fillies back from a forge
Newly shod, to wake me at sunrise from a single bed
With laughter peeling skin from a dream ripening on the mossy
Branches of my head—'Let us in! Let us in!'—and half-naked
I stumble over a floor of heaped paper to open my door of
    glass
To a flood that crosses the threshold, little blue waves

Nudging each other, dodging rocks they've got to leap over,
Freshening my brackish pools, to tell me of 'O such a night
Below in the boats!' 'We can't go home! What *will* they say?'
Can I think of a lie to protect them from God only knows
What trouble this will cause, what rows? 'We'll run away
And never come back!'—till they flop into black armchairs,
Two beautiful teenage girls from a tribe of tinkers,

Lovely as seals wet from fishing, hauled out on a rock
To dry their dark brown fur glinting with scales of salmon
When the spring tide ebbs. This is their everlasting day
Of being young. They bring to my room the sea's iodine
    odour
On a breeze of voices ruffling my calm as they comb their long
Hair tangled as weed in a rockpool beginning to settle clear.
Give me the sea-breath from your mouths to breathe a while!

TONY WHITE
1930–1976

Growing, he saw his friends increase
Their incomes, houses, families,
And saw this growth as a disease
Nothing but unpossessive love could cure.

Possessing nothing, he was not possessed
By things or people, as we are.
His granite chimney breast
Warmed friend or stranger at its open fire.
There was no air
Too foul for him to breathe, no pit
Too dark to enter, yet
His very breathing made the foul air pure,
His presence made the darkest day feel clear.

He lived at the hub and not the rim
Of time. Within himself he moved
Deeper towards dangerous ideas he loved
To moot with bodily risk:
Flying too close to the sun's disk,
Sailing at night over a coral reef,
Ghosting a thief's life.
Since he's gone
No words of mine can rivet him to one
Role of some forty-nine he used to play
For pleasure more than pay.
Because his kind of love taught me to live
His dying I forgive.

GYM

Vice-regal walls dominate the back street
Where men, succumbing to my spurious name
For body culture, enter in retreat
From words that shame, to act a heartless mime.

Discreetly couched, taking no verbal risk,
Ingled in clutches masked by sauna steam,
Nude club members, immune from women, bask
In tableaux mixed with musak, cocaine, jism.

See how my fabric, full of cock and bull,
Grotesquely free, though ruled by symmetry,
Lays you in some small penetralian cell
To come to grief, past all immunity.

The powers that be, served covertly by aids,
Strip to the bone your skin-deep masquerades.

ELIXIR

Turning a stone house into seven figures
Transported him to money's clean cold alp
To hang-glide on a market's thermal rigours
Learning new ways to corner, hedge or scalp.

Turning a copper nail that tightly gripped
A green slate on his roof to daily bread
Made him afraid to eat when sterling dipped
And meat cost more than door locks or sheet lead.

Turning a life's work into stocks and shares
Converted him to shirk the tears and shocks
Of love, rid of laborious household cares
And freed him to buy sex on piers and docks.

Turning old granite walls to bars of gold
Amassed his fears of sudden falls in one
Commodity. When all his wealth was told
It filled a vault with bone-dry speculation.

Turning his home into a foreign room
Replete with art to beat inflation chilled
His heart to zero. In that ice-bound tomb
He housed immortal seed unsowed, untilled.

ROOF-TREE

After you brought her home with your first child
How did you celebrate? Not with a poem
She might have loved, but orders to rebuild
The house. Men tore me open, room by room.

Your daughter's cries were answered by loud cracks
Of hammers stripping slates; the clawing down
Of dozed rafters; dull, stupefying knocks
On walls. Proudly your hackwork made me groan.

Your greed for kiln-dried oak that could outlast
Seven generations broke her heart. My mind
You filled with rot-proof hemlock at a cost
That killed her love. The dust spread unrefined.

To renovate my structure, which survives,
You flawed the tenderest movement of three lives.

Thomas Kinsella

b. 1928

from A TECHNICAL SUPPLEMENT

IV

The point, greatly enlarged,
pushed against the skin
depressing an area of tissue.
Rupture occurred: at first a separation
at the intensest place among the cells
then a deepening damage
with nerve-strings fraying
and snapping and writhing back.
Blood welled up to fill the wound,
bathing the point as it went deeper.

Persist.
        Beyond a certain depth
it stands upright by itself
and quivers with borrowed life.

Persist.
        And you may find
the buried well. And take on
the stillness of a root.

Quietus.
        Or:

V

A blade licks out and acts
with one tongue.
Jets of blood respond

32

in diverse tongues.
And promptly.
A single sufficient cut
and the body drops at once.
No reserve. Inert.

If you would care to enter this grove of beasts:

VI

A veteran smiled and let us pass through
to the dripping groves in Swift's slaughterhouse,
hot confusion and the scream-rasp of the saw.
Huge horned fruit not quite dead
—chained, hooked by one hock, stunned
above a pool of steaming spiceblood.

Two elderly men in aprons waded back and forth
with long knives they sharpened slowly and
inserted, tapping cascades of black blood
that collapsed before their faces onto the concrete.
Another fallen beast landed, kicking,
and was hooked by the ankle and hoisted into its place.

They come in behind a plank barrier on an upper level
walking with erect tail to the stunning place . . .
Later in the process they encounter
a man who loosens the skin around their tails
with deep cuts in unexpected directions;
the tail springs back; the hide pulls down to the jaws.

With the sheep it was even clearer
they were dangling alive, the blood trickling
over nostrils and teeth. A flock of them waited their turn
crowded into the furthest corner of the pen,
some looking back over their shoulders
at us, in our window.

Great bulks of pigs hung from dainty heels,
the full sow-throats cut open the wrong way.
Three negroes stood on a raised bench before them.
One knifed the belly open upward to the tail
until the knife and his hands disappeared
in the fleshy vulva and broke some bone.

The next opened it downward to the throat,
embraced the mass of entrails, lifted them out
and dropped them in a chute. And so to one
who excavated the skull through flaps of the face,
hooked it onto the carcase and pushed all forward
toward a frame of blue flames, the singeing machine.

At a certain point it is all merely meat,
sections hung or stacked in a certain order.
Downstairs a row of steel barrows
holds the liquid heaps of organs.
As each new piece drops, adding itself,
the contents tremble throughout their mass.

In a clean room a white-coated worker
positioned a ham, found a blood vessel with a forceps,
clipped it to a tube of red chemical
and pumped the piece full. It swelled immediately
and saturated: tiny crimson jets
poured from it everywhere. Transfused!

VII

Vital spatterings. Excess.
Make the mind creep. Play-blood
bursting everywhere out of
big chopped dolls: the stuff breaking copiously
out of a slow, horrified head.

Is it all right to do this?
Is it an offence against justice

34

when someone stumbles away helplessly
and has to sit down
until her sobbing stops?

VIII

How to put it ... without offence
—even though it is an offence,
monstrous, in itself.

A living thing swallowing another.

Lizards:
   Stone still
holding it sideways in its jaws.
With a jerk, adjusting it
with the head facing nearer.

The two staring in separate directions.

Again. The head inside the mouth
and the little hands and feet and the tail
and the suddenly soft round belly
hanging down outside.
        Again.
Splayed hind legs and a tail.

A tail.
   Then
a leather-granite face
unfulfillable.

IX

A dark hall. Great green liquid windows
lit. The Stations of the Depths.

In its deep tank, a leopard shark patrolled
away from the window, enlarging to a shadow.
It circled back, grew brighter, reduced
into blunt focus—a pink down-laugh, white needles—
and darkened away again, lengthening.

A herring-flock pelted in spinning water
staring in place—they trembled with speed
and fled, shifted and corrected,
strung together invisibly in their cluster.

Two morays craned up their exposed shoulders
from a cleft, the bird-beaked heads
peering up at a far off music of slaughter,
moving with it, thick and stiff.

A still tank. Gross anemones flowered open
flesh-brilliant on slopes of rock.
A crayfish, crusted with black detail, dreamed
on twig tips across the bottom sand.
A crab fumbled at the lip of a coral shelf
and a gentle fish cruised outward, and down.

ARTISTS' LETTERS

Folders, papers, proofs, maps
with tissue paper marked and coloured.
I was looking for something,
confirmation of something,
in the cardboard box
when my fingers deflected among
fat packets of love letters,
old immediacies in elastic bands.

I shook a letter open from
its creases, carefully, and read
—and shrugged, embarrassed.
                                        Then stirred.
My hand grew thin and agitated
as the words crawled again
quickly over the dried paper.

Letter by letter the foolishness
deepened, but displayed
a courage in its own unsureness;
acknowledged futility and waste
in all their importance . . . a young idiocy
in desperate full-hearted abandon
to all the chance of one choice:

There is one throw, no more. One
offering: make it. With no style
—these are desperate times. There is
a poverty of spirit in the wind,
a shabby richness in braving it.
My apologies, but you are my beloved
and I will not be put off.

What is it about such letters,
torn free ignominiously
in love? Character stripped off
our pens plunge repeatedly
at the unique cliché, cover
ache after ache of radiant paper
with analytic ecstasies,
wrestle in repetitious fury.

The flesh storms our brain; we storm
our entranced opposite, badger her
with body metaphors, project

our selves with outthrust stuttering arms,
cajoling, forcing her
—her spread-eagled spirit—
to accept our suspect cries
with shocked and shining eyes.

Artists' letters (as the young career
grows firmer in excited pride
and moves toward authority
after the first facetiousness,
the spirit shaken into strength
by shock after shock of understanding)
suddenly shudder and *display*! Animal.
Violent vital organs of desire.

A toothless mouth opens
and we throw ourselves, enthralled, against our bonds
and thrash toward her. And when we have
been nicely eaten and our parts
spat out whole and have become
'one', *then* we can settle our cuffs
and our Germanic collar
and turn back calmly toward distinguished things.

THE FURNACE

Imperishable creatures
returning into God's light.
A resurrection, not a vanishing.

Intensifying, as iron
melts in the furnace
—intensified into flowing fire,

aching for a containing Shape.
Eriugena's notion matching
my half-baked, bodily own,

who have *consigned*
my designing will stonily
to your flames

and will turn again toward the same furnace
that melted the union of our will
to ineffable zero

how many times in its radiant clasp
(a cancellation
certainly speechless for a minute or two)

in token of the Union and the Light.
Until gender returned
and we were made two again

Male and Female
in punishment for Man's will
and reminded of our Fall.

In token of which
I plant this dry kiss
in your rain-wet hair.

John Montague

b. 1929

A FLOWERING ABSENCE

How can one make an absence flower,
lure a desert to sudden bloom?
Taut with terror, I rehearse a time
when I was taken from a sick room:
as before from your flayed womb.

And given away to be fostered
wherever charity could afford.
I came back, lichened with sores,
from the care of still poorer
immigrants, new washed from the hold.

I bless their unrecorded names,
whose need was greater than mine,
wet nurses from tenement darkness
giving suck for a time,
because their milk was plentiful

Or their own children gone.
They were the first to succour
that still terrible thirst of mine,
a thirst for love and knowledge,
to learn something of that time

Of confusion, poverty, absence.
Year by year, I track it down
intent for a hint of evidence,
seeking to manage the pain—
how a mother gave away her son.

I took the subway to the hospital
in darkest Brooklyn, to call
on the old nun who nursed you
through the travail of my birth
to come on another cold trail.

Sister Virgilius, how strange!
She died, just before you came.
She was delirious, rambling of all
her old patients; she could well
have remembered your mother's name.

Around the bulk of St. Catherine's
another wild, raunchier Brooklyn:
as tough a territory as I've known,
strutting young Puerto Rican hoods,
flash of blade, of bicycle chain.

Mother, my birth was the death
of your love life, the last man
to flutter near your tender womb:
a neonlit barsign winks off & on,
motherfucka, thass your name.

There is an absence, real as presence.
In the mornings I hear my daughter
chuckle, with runs of sudden joy.
Hurt, she rushes to her mother,
as I never could, a whining boy.

All roads wind backwards to it.
An unwanted child, a primal hurt.
I caught fever on the big boat
that brought us away from America
—away from my lost parents.

Surely my father loved me,
teaching me to croon, *Ragtime Cowboy
Joe, swaying in his saddle
as he sings*, as he did, drunkenly
dropping in from the speakeasy.

So I found myself shipped back
to his home, in an older country,
transported to a previous century,
where his sisters restored me,
natural love flowering around me.

And the hurt ran briefly underground
to break out in a schoolroom
where I was taunted by a mistress
who hunted me publicly down
to near speechlessness.

*So this is our brightest infant?
Where did he get that outlandish accent?
What do you expect, with no parents,
sent back from some American slum:
none of you are to speak like him!*

Stammer, impediment, stutter:
she had found my lode of shame,
and soon I could no longer utter
those magical words I had begun
to love, to dolphin delight in.

And not for two stumbling decades
would I manage to speak straight again.
Grounded for the second time
my tongue became a rusted hinge
until the sweet oils of poetry

eased it and light flooded in.

THE LOCKET

Sing a last song
for the lady who has gone,
fertile source of guilt and pain.
The worst birth in the annals of Brooklyn,
that was my cue to come on,
my first claim to fame.

Naturally, she longed for a girl,
and all my infant curls of brown
couldn't excuse my double blunder
coming out, both the wrong sex,
and the wrong way around.
Not readily forgiven

So you never nursed me
and when all my father's songs
couldn't sweeten the lack of money,
when poverty comes through the door
love flies up the.chimney,
your favourite saying,

Then you gave me away,
might never have known me,
if I had not cycled down
to court you like a young man,
teasingly untying your apron,
drinking by the fire, yarning

Of your wild, young days
which didn't last long, for you,
lovely Molly, the belle of your small town,
landed up mournful and chill
as the constant rain that lashes it,
wound into your cocoon of pain.

Standing in that same hallway,
don't come again, you say, roughly,
I start to get fond of you, John,
and then you are up and gone;
the harsh logic of a forlorn woman
resigned to being alone.

And still, mysterious blessing,
I never knew, until you were gone,
that, always around your neck,
you wore an oval locket
with an old picture in it,
of a child in Brooklyn.

THE WELL-BELOVED

To wake up and discover—
a splurge of chill water—
that she was but a forthright woman
on whom we had bestowed
(because of the crook of an elbow,
the swing of a breast or hip,
a glance half understood)
divinity or angelhood?

Raised by the fury of our need,
supplicating, lusting, grovelling
before the tall tree of Artemis,
the transfiguring bow of Diana,
the rooting vulva of Circe, or
the slim shape of a nymph,
luring, dancing, beckoning:
all her wild disguises!

And now she does not shine,
or ride, like the full moon,
gleam or glisten like cascades
of uncatchable, blinding water;
disturb like the owl's cry
by night, predatory, hovering;
marshlight, moonstone, or devil's daughter.
But conducts herself like any

Normal citizen, orderly or slattern,
giving us a piece of her mind,
pacifying or scolding children,
or, more determinedly, driving
or riding to her office, after
depositing the children in a *crêche*,
while she fulfills herself,
competing with the best.

Of course, she is probably saying
the same thing of us, as Oisin,
our tall hero from Fairyland,
descends or falls from the saddle
to dwindle into an irritable husband,
worn down by the quotidian,
unwilling to transform the night
with love's necessary shafts of light.

Except that when the old desires stir
—fish under weed-tangled waters—
will she remember that we once were
the strange ones who understood
the powers that coursed so furiously
through her witch blood, prepared
to stand, bareheaded, open handed,
to recognise, worship and obey:

To defy custom, redeem the ordinary,
with trembling heart, and obeisant knee
to kneel, prostrate ourselves again,
if necessary, before the lady?

MOUNT EAGLE

I

The eagle looked at this changing world;
sighed and disappeared into the mountain.

Before he left he had a last reconnoitre:
the multi-coloured boats in the harbour

Nodded their masts, and a sandy white
crescent of strand smiled back at him.

How he liked the slight, drunk lurch
of the fishing fleet, the tide hoist-

ing them a little, at their ropes' end.
Beyond, wrack, and the jutting rocks

emerging, slowly, monsters stained
and slimed with strands of seaweed.

Ashore, beached boats and lobster
pots, settled as hens in the sand.

II

Content was life in its easiest form;
another was the sudden, growling storm

which the brooding eagle preferred
bending his huge wings into the winds'

wild buffeting, or thrusting down along
the wide sky, at an angle, slideways to

survey the boats, scurrying homewards,
tacking against the now contrary winds,

all of whom he knew by their names.
To be angry in the morning, calmed

by midday, but brooding again in
the evening was all in a day's quirk

with lengthy intervals for silence,
gliding along, like a blessing, while

the fleet toiled on earnestly beneath
him, bulging with a fine day's catch.

III

But now he had to enter the mountain.
Why? Because a cliff had asked him?
The whole world was changing, with one
language dying, and another encroaching,
bright with buckets, cries of children.
There seemed to be no end to them,
and the region needed a guardian—
so the mountain had told him. And

A different destiny lay before him:
to be the spirit of that mountain.
Everyone would stand in awe of him.
When he was wrapped in the mist's caul
they would withdraw because of him,

peer from behind blind, or curtain.
When he lifted his wide forehead
bold with light, in the morning,
they would all laugh and smile with him.
It was a greater task than an eagle's
aloofness, but sometimes, under his oilskin
of coiled mist, he sighed for lost freedom.

CASSANDRA'S ANSWER

I

All I can do is curse, complain.
I told you the flames would come
and the small towns blaze. Though

Precious little you did about it!
Obdurate. Roots are obstructions
as well as veins of growth.

How my thick tongue longs
for honey's ease, the warm
full syllables of praise.

Instead of this gloomy procession
of casualties, clichés of disease:
deaf mutes' clamouring palms.

To have one subject only,
fatal darkness of prophecy,
gaunt features always veiled.

I have forgotton how I sang
as a young girl, before my voice
changed, and I tolled funerals.

I feel my mouth grow heavy again.
a storm cloud is sailing in:
a street will receive its viaticum

In the fierce release of a bomb.
(Good-bye, Main Street, Fintona.
good-bye to the old Carney home.)

II

To step inside a childhood home,
tattered rafters that the dawn
leaks through, brings awareness

Bleaker than any you have known.
Whole albums of births, marriages,
roomfuls of tears and loving confidences

Gone as if the air had swallowed them:
stairs which climb towards nothing,
walls hosed down to flaking stone:

you were born inside a skeleton.

SHE CRIES

She puts her face against the wall
and cries, crying for herself,
crying for our children, crying
for all of us
                in this strange age
of shrinking space, with the needle
of Concorde saluting Mount Gabriel
with its supersonic boom, soaring

from London or Paris to Washington,
a slender, metallic, flying swan

& all other paraphernalia, hidden
missiles hoarded in silos, bloated
astronauts striding the dusty moon,
and far beyond, our lonely message,
the long probe towards Venus

but most of all for her husband
she cries, against the wall,
the poet at his wooden desk,
that toad with a jewel in his head,
no longer privileged, but still
trying to crash, without faltering,
the sound barrier, the dying word.

Sean Lucy

b. 1930

MISSING LINK

You must admit the loss of blood, brother:
old Ireland held huge herds—safe in her plains and glens
between rivers and deep woods—
huge wealth of meat and milk and leather,
the bulls bred for the kings, the kings fed the kin;
acorn rich pigs' blood

filled the big puddings; the foaming fleece of sheep
from steeper places took tone from saffron, woad, and alder.
It was all our own.
And the love felt for the animals ran deep:
even as they fed us, they were us; it was no murder,
they were our flesh and bone.

Now we sell much meat to strangers; my own grandfather
was a cattle-dealer. Not just meat, moaning herds
like a muddy river to the shore
have drained into slave-ships for generations.
The tribes are broken.
                    The sacred words
between man and own animal are not heard anymore.

James Simmons

b. 1933

FOR THOMAS MOORE

When the young have grown tired
and the old are abused,
when beauty's degraded
and brilliance not used,
when courage is clumsy
and strength misapplied
we wish that our seed
in the dark womb had died.

But when youth finds its singers
and old men find peace
and beauty finds servants
and genius, release,
when courage has wisdom
and strength mends our wrongs
we will sing unembarrassed
your marvellous songs.

CLAUDY
For Harry Barton

(song)

The Sperrins surround it, the Faughan flows by,
at each end of Main Street the hills and the sky,
the small town of Claudy at ease in the sun
last July in the morning, a new day begun.

How peaceful and pretty if the moment could stop,
McIlhenny is straightening things in his shop,
and his wife is outside serving petrol, and then
a girl takes a cloth to a big window pane.

And McCloskey is taking the weight off his feet,
and McClelland and Miller are sweeping the street,
and, delivering milk at the Beaufort Hotel,
young Temple's enjoying his first job quite well.

And Mrs. McLaughlin is scrubbing her floor,
and Artie Hone's crossing the street to a door,
and Mrs. Brown, looking around for her cat,
goes off up an entry—what's strange about that?

Not much—but before she comes back to the road
that strange car parked outside her house will explode,
and all of the people I've mentioned outside
will be waiting to die or already have died.

An explosion too loud for your ear drums to bear,
and young children squealing like pigs in the square,
and all faces chalk white and streaked with bright red,
and the glass and the dust and the terrible dead.

For an old lady's legs are ripped off, and the head
of a man's hanging open, and still he's not dead.
He is screaming for mercy, and his son stands and
            stares
and stares, and then suddenly, quick, disappears.

And Christ, little Katharine Aikin is dead,
and Mrs. McLaughlin is pierced through the head.
Meanwhile to Dungiven the killers have gone,
and they're finding it hard to get through on the phone.

OCTOBER IN THE COUNTRY

'What you can suffer you can sing.'

Wind shakes my window frames
with an empty afternoon roar,
and that damned born-again Christian
is out riding his lawn-mower.

His garden is cluttered with dormobiles,
power-boats of glossy fibreglass,
hedge-cutters, rotivators, vans:
the expensive hobbies of a pain-in-the-ass.

And the farmer whose cowshed spoils our view,
whose poisonous leaking silage destroys
black currant bushes and rhubarb clumps,
whose presence is always stink and noise,

is pumping his foul slurry and racing
backwards and forwards to his fields,
mechanically incontinent
in hot pursuit of higher yields.

We hear his crammed uneasy cattle
shifting and groaning in the barn all night
in winter, heads stuck out through bars,
up to their knees in their own shite.

This is my refuge, my countryside!
Yet, believe it or not, to speak the truth
I am happier here in my middle-years
than ever I was in my Derry youth.

The only material for jokes
is annoyances. The cruel course

of our human race has been fixed for us
democratically: damned at the source

but improving, maybe. I give my vote
to reformers; but setting the cattle free
and driving South to the Sperrins? No.
We'd be caught, and cattle frighten me.

I have lit the fire and closed the shutters
against noisy gardeners and farmers.
The votive light in my amplifier
draws me to worship some great performers.

James Liddy

b. 1934

DONAGH MacDONAGH

"So small and young" the silver moon with its spoons hung
in the Dublin hills skyway glasslayer before World War One
I admired the acidity of his effulgence in the bar of White's Hotel
or in Groome's on a still born rose Fianna Fail morning
he was the well of rebellion well splashed with Thwaite's soda
    water

pieces of ice rattled in his cup and down his spine
the foggy country of holy wells that had lashing tongues
had carpeted into an over-behaving lounge boy sank down
to girl in mute beastliness, no behaving-bred eloquence—
that sparkled his ire and the longing inside us to be English.
he was not Alexander Pope nor was meant to be
one that bandaged up his wound in super rhyming couplets
and ate a super supper in a nice place

though he coupleted a piece about the Botanic Gardens
more artificial than any 18th century poem about flowers. . . .
The cattle still moved on the roads of Wexford against the
    cars
the tinkers silverbelling their fists and feet
sang from flagon to flagon of Bulmers like king's children
he noted them in his book of records not in his Court book
whose fines he sang out like lines of a verse play before a
    sergeant
had time to complete the names of the defendants.
The first drizzly day he drove to Gorey to take the Court
the town's street saw his wife wear no stockings—bare legs—
and knew they were bad ones, denizens of Bohemia's
untameable storm clad luxurious sea sands.

II

I know nothing but this scene:
a farmer's field of grass
stalky and thistledowned
buttercups
cowslips
belladona-standing hedges—
an edge of sadness
... ghosts a
thousand years of horses ...
and a trampled section a swath
of a path on one side,
the one with running water,
no trees except on the far bank
(to swim in it naked for even a few minutes)
A slightly tilting field
on the road to Limerick
called Barrington's Bridge (I am sure)
with access to the wandering slithering
thickening slendering Maigue
to which the bards of Desmond brought,
tramping through the ragwort,
their narcissistic fears like piss
standing on the bank on their big feet
singly or monkey-chattering
until in the cool of evening—
if they came then—without caves
teeth-chattering started.

Anxiety the stalks running
through my body about the past
that is swept away like the Maigue
swept on by spring flood,
no punctuation no looking back.
(To swim in it, a fish in water.)
One sentence on it runs into another,

another bardic figure round the bend
or—what we want—a sensuous body
round the corner beckoning.

The dream bard out of the hedge
stands on the edge
and dissolves into poetry . . .
splashes a young nubile figure
in the parting stream.
My tired eye focuses there
the sensuous flesh becoming
non-bachelor wonder-past—
the river murmurs through its green
sludge. . . .
A near naked army may
Have stood on either side
Pre-demon fighting with demon . . .
nothing carries your eye
back further than the blink of a river.
I place my arms around nakedness
Meaning comes on like evening.
It was an outing: frisky lambkins
recovered from breakfast
and cigarette-walk on the terrace
rampageous pigeons uncaged
blurring along the field path, for
a sports meeting then a picnic.
The under-14 hundred yards
a handicap event and I was a few
yards in front . . . togged out.
A start gun held by Fr. Peter
for the hopping-flopping bunch . . .
I looked at the river at the trees
I saw the demons hovering
over the water—bridegrooms . . .
I decided to run (pounding temple
prickly arse) and poured over

the line first, a cheered hero.
One to whom men would speak . . .
a swan sailed by the river
singing like a bard on his death bed
like a bard who has been to the river
for the last time. O swept away too
the warm summer of Pius XII
as hot as the Campagna . . .
though a camoufleur I had run
like one of those over the flat grass
in the fields aside Anacotty
for the gold medal and I seemed
not like one who loses but
like one who's won.

I learnt to sing (thank you)
and I sing before the painted
marriage chamber door.
By song not restoring the past
(puberty, the river, the garland
that is a lost medal)—
it's not even a task.
The initiation is to transfer sexual
purpose—everything that is energy—
into the creative not the sublime.
To be-bop more of a lover as you
incarnate better the poet.
To be flowing more of a river sensualist.

Desmond O'Grady

b. 1935

BERLIN METRO

Every year they try to rob us
of our Mediterranean minds.
Watch out, friend, for fields
of false foreign promises from afar.
They forget we may pirouette
across the Pyrenees of imagination,
for our own George Sands who came
from nowhere, to play our pianos
for Amir Ahmed and Mahmoud Darwish,
Salah Abd al-Sabir and Yehuda Amichai
for northern Derek Mahon, southern O'Grady
at U.N. 242 because we may never return.
We must confront our common grief
of Beirut, Belfast, Jerusalem and pray
to Saint Sam Beckett to guide us safe.
They must allow us free to play provincial
conkers, knucklebones, the three-card trick
by Hadrian's Wall while they deliberate decisions
at the Synod of Whitby. We'll anyway highland
fling the Christos' Chinese Wall and sing ballads
back and forth across the Mason-Dixon line for peace.
We shall always grope our way along the Berlin Corridor.
The mitred Magician's Polish mission
Vaticinates Finlandisation for now while we
anguish an old Viking ferocity come back
to desecrate the land of our disinherited ancestors,
witness renewed barbarian invasions across the Alps
again each summer to desecrate the values of Europe.
A Hollywood horizon dawns white as decalcinated bones
Daedalus unravels Penelope's labyrinth

and Hektor, stood apart from his woman and son,
observes sardonically from the high wall of his Troy.
Fog is general all over the west. Odysseus weeps
alone at the first stone of Jericho. Mythology's
mask hangs crucified for the price of a government pension.
Bruno Hoffman plays Mozart's Glass Harmonica unheeded.
Yesterday I read blindly in the Torah, Koran, Bible
and everywhere saw the cloven hoofprint of tomorrow's
   Sitting Bull.

after Thomas Venclova

TIPPERARY

It's a long way to Tipperary
It's a long way to go—and devious.
It's a torture of twists, about-turns,
disillusions, disappointments.
The way to Tipperary appears
perennially dark with only
occasional twilights.

If you decide to go to Tipperary
set out while you're young, plucky;
at that age when you're bright-eyed with visions
of radiant horizons of revelation and achievement
and you know nothing of twilights or the dark,
that age when all creation, all life shines clear
as spring sunlight, bright as light catching gold.

When you set out you must go alone.
There are no maps of the way to Tipperary.
Your only compass is your own heart.
Trust that!

Some see their Tipperary clearly from the start;
see it's a long road, full of daily pitfalls,
a confusing labyrinth of curious sidestreets, inviting
guesthouses; giddy with the temptations, distractions
of those bogey people's trinket stalls, hokey-pokey-
daily thieves of eternal energy—easy come, easy go,
you've sold your soul, you've no more choice.
They sell bedlam!

Explore all those sidestreets,
enjoy your chosen resthouses,
fool with a few trinkets to learn
something of the capricious way to
Tipperary.

The way to Tipperary's dark with the shadows of those
who never got there anyway; those who settled
for some resthouse, some trinket thief of time.
Don't let those shadows, mumbling in their own gloom,
deter or deviate you. Hold the main road. Keep going!

Once you've decided to go to Tipperary
you'll realize you no longer belong to yourself
but must keep Tipperary in your sights daily—
although you can't see it. Purpose is all.
Without your Tipperary you too are a mere shadow
at those Limerick Junctions of daily resolution.

On the way to Tipperary keep your eye open
for signals of direction, encouragement:
that nod of understanding, comradeship of commitment;
a gentle arm on your pillow that cherishes. You'll see
beautiful sights on the way to Tipperary:
man's mirage tales, imagination's monuments.
You'll behold the endless vistas, expansive panoramas,
seas and deserts of vision. Be curious about them all

for the gracious gifts they will afford you.
Without them you'd live that much the poorer.

It's a long way to Tipperary
and when you get there
nothing awaits you. You'll find no roadsign,
no brassband and welcoming committee
with a banner proclaiming you're in Tipperary
and a medallion to hang around your neck.
You'll find only what you brought with you
in your heart.

Then, what you must do
is make and leave some record
of what your Tipperary means to you—
as witness for all those behind you
on their ways to their own Tipperaries.

It's a long way to Tipperary
and all our hearts lie there.

Note: Tipperary: English for Irish *Tiobraid Arann: Tiobraid:* fountain, well, spring. *Arann:* intelligence, perception. *Tiobraidarann:* the fountain of perception.

Brendan Kennelly

b. 1936

MASTER

"I am master of the chivalric idiom" Spenser said
As he sipped a jug of buttermilk
And ate a quaite of griddle bread.
"I'm worried, though, about the actual bulk
Of *The Faerie Queene*. She's growing out
Of all proportions, in different directions.
Am I losing control? Am I buggering it
All up? Ruining my best intentions?
As relief from my Queene, I write sonnets
But even these little things get out of hand
Now and then, giving me a nightmare head.
Trouble is, sonnets are genetic epics.
Something in them wants to grow out of bounds.
I'm up to my bollox in sonnets" Spenser said.

THE POSITION OF PRAISE

"Praise God" said Spenser, "You live where you choose,
Buffún. I'm not in love with Cork even
Though I enjoy all these pleasant Sundays
When I stand apart and watch the Corkmen
Lofting the viaduct. No, friends shoved me
Over here because I loved green tables
And round tables and gentle chivalry.
I would halt these coarse tides drowning
England but all a poet can be to-day
Is witness to ambitious ugliness
Disfiguring the old and graceful ways.

Since they have made an outcast of me
I know that I, in Cork, must always bless
Whoever mauls England. They maim. I praise."

IN THE SEA

Big Island whispered to little island
"I'm right here at your back.
Shall I bugger you?
Shall I breathe down your neck?
Most of the time I hardly see you at all
You're so small, you're so small
And when you insist that you really exist
I can scarcely follow your voice.
Well, do you exist, you sea-shrouded mite?
Or are you a floating illusion
Invisible to all except me?"

Little island replied "There is sea-light
Between us, and storms and countless drowned men.
Yes, I'm near you. Near. Right here. In the sea."

A WOUND

Little island whispered over his shoulder
To Big Island who was reflecting on
The fact that there was no island more
Beautiful than himself, "I'm here, and someone,

Probably one of my aboriginals,
Has set out in a low boat bearing proof
Of this. You may boot him in the genitals,
Work him over, lock him up, but his love

For me is such he believes I exist
And wishes to remind you of that truth."
A bomb mashed Big Island in the side,

The aboriginal was duly booted and later lost.
"I'm here" said little island. "I can see that"
Groaned Big, "I must tend this wound before it goes bad."

PLANS

William of Orange was always worried
About the state of the Gross National Product.
"Unless the G.N.P. improves" he said
To a seminar in Listowel, "We're fucked!

I've been looking around at this island
And it's clear to me the major industry
Is holiness. The people's souls are sound.
I note a link between holiness and money.

I'm drawing up plans for a factory
Where I shall manufacture rosary-beads.
About a million tourists blow this way

Each year to view our native sanctity.
God is telling us to use our heads.
Holiness is thriving, lads. Let's make it pay."

A RUNNING BATTLE

What are they doing now? I imagine Oliver
Buying a Dodge, setting up as a taxi-driver
Shunting three dozen farmers to Listowel Races.

I see Ed Spenser, father of all our graces
In verse, enshrined as a knife-minded auctioneer
Addicted to Woodbines and Kilkenny beer,
Selling Parish Priests' shiny furniture
To fox-eyed housewives and van-driving tinkers.
William of Orange is polishing pianos
In convents and other delicate territories,
His nose purple from sipping turpentine.
Little island is Big, Big Island is little.
I never knew a love that wasn't a running battle
Most of the time. I'm a friend of these ghosts. They're mine.

from Cromwell (1983)

Seamus Heaney

b. 1939

FUNERAL RITES

I

I shouldered a kind of manhood
stepping in to lift the coffins
of dead relations.
They had been laid out

in tainted rooms,
their eyelids glistening,
their dough-white hands
shackled in rosary beads.

Their puffed knuckles
had unwrinkled, the nails
were darkened, the wrists
obediently sloped.

The dulse-brown shroud,
the quilted satin cribs:
I knelt courteously
admiring it all

as wax melted down
and veined the candles,
the flames hovering
to the women hovering

behind me.
And always, in a corner,

the coffin lid,
its nail-heads dressed

with little gleaming crosses.
Dear soapstone masks,
kissing their igloo brows
had to suffice

before the nails were sunk
and the black glacier
of each funeral
pushed away.

II

Now as news comes in
of each neighbourly murder
we pine for ceremony,
customary rhythms:

the temperate footsteps
of a cortège, winding past
each blinded home.
I would restore

the great chambers of Boyne,
prepare a sepulchre
under the cupmarked stones.
Out of side-streets and bye-roads

purring family cars
nose into line,
the whole country tunes
to the muffled drumming

of ten thousand engines.
Somnambulant women,

left behind, move
through emptied kitchens

imagining our slow triumph
towards the mounds.
Quiet as a serpent
in its grassy boulevard

the procession drags its tail
out of the Gap of the North
as its head already enters
the megalithic doorway.

III

When they have put the stone
back in its mouth
we will drive north again
past Strang and Carling fjords

the cud of memory
allayed for once, arbitration
of the feud placated,
imagining those under the hill

disposed like Gunnar
who lay beautiful
inside his burial mound,
though dead by violence

and unavenged.
Men said that he was chanting
verses about honour
and that four lights burned

in corners of the chamber:
which opened then, as he turned

with a joyful face
to look at the moon.

THE HARVEST BOW

As you plaited the harvest bow
You implicated the mellowed silence in you
In wheat that does not rust
But brightens as it tightens twist by twist
Into a knowable corona,
A throwaway love-knot of straw.

Hands that aged round ashplants and cane sticks
And lapped the spurs on a lifetime of game cocks
Harked to their gift and worked with fine intent
Until your fingers moved somnambulant:
I tell and finger it like braille,
Cleaning the unsaid off the palpable,

And if I spy into its golden loops
I see us walk between the railway slopes
Into an evening of long grass and midges,
Blue smoke straight up, old beds and ploughs in hedges,
An auction notice on an outhouse wall—
You with a harvest bow in your lapel,

Me with the fishing rod, already homesick
For the big lift of these evenings, as your stick
Whacking the tips off weeds and bushes
Beats out of time, and beats, but flushes
Nothing: that original townland
Still tongue-tied in the straw tied by your hand.

The end of art is peace
Could be the motto of this frail device

That I have pinned up on our deal dresser—
Like a drawn snare
Slipped lately by the spirit of the corn
Yet burnished by its passage, and still warm.

THE ASH PLANT

He'll never rise again but he is ready.
Entered like a mirror by the morning,
He stares out the big window, wondering,
Not caring if the day is bright or cloudy.

An upstairs outlook on the whole country.
First milk lorries, first smoke, Friesians, trees
In damp opulence above the hedges—
He has it to himself, he is like a sentry

Forgotten and unable to remember
The whys and wherefores of his lofty station,
Wakening relieved yet in position,
Disencumbered as a breaking comber.

As his head goes light with light, his wasting hand
Gropes desperately and finds the phantom limb
Of an ash plant in his grasp, which steadies him.
Now he has found his touch he can stand his ground

Or wield the stick like a silver bough and come
Walking again among us: the quoted judge.
I could have cut a better man out of the hedge!
God might have thought the same, remembering Adam.

THE SCHOOLBAG

i.m. JOHN HEWITT

My handsewn leather schoolbag. Forty years.
Poet, you were *nel mezzo del cammin*
When I shouldered it, half-full of blue-lined jotters,
And saw the classroom charts, the displayed bean,
The wall-map with its spray of shipping lanes
Describing arcs across the blue North Channel . . .
And in the middle of the road to school,
Ox-eye daisies and wild dandelions.

Learning's easy carried! The bag is light,
Scuffed and supple and unemptiable
As an itinerant school-conjuror's hat.
So take it, for your word-hoard and your handsel,
As you step out, trig as ever, behind weavers,
Journeymen, spalpeens and cattle-drovers.

THE DARK WOOD
for Derry Jeffares

In the middle of the journey of our life
I discovered myself in a dark wood
Where the straight road had been lost sight of.

Ah, it is hard to say how gnarled and strong
And full of thickets it was in that wood
I panic even now remembering.

It is bitter almost as the taste of death.
But to rehearse the good that came of it
For me, I will tell the other things I met with.

How I got into it I cannot clearly say
For I was moving like a sleepwalker
The moment I stepped out of the right way

But when I came to the foot of a hill
That stood at the far end of that valley
Where my heart had begun to fear and tremble

I looked up, and saw its shoulders glowed
Already in the rays of the planet
Which leads and keeps men straight on every road.

Then I sensed a quiet settling
Into those depths in me that had been rocked
And pitifully troubled all night long,

And as a survivor gasping on the sand
Turns his head back to study in a daze
The dangerous combers, so my mind

Turned back, although it was reeling still,
To inspect that gap no one ever entered
And came out again alive to tell the tale.

I rested a little then for I was tired
And began to climb up the waste slopes once more,
With my lower foot always my best support,

When suddenly the spotted fluent shape
Of a leopard crossed my path
Not far up from the bottom of the slope,

Harrying me, confronting my advance,
Loping round me, leaping in my face
So that I turned back downhill more than once.

The morning was beginning all above,
The sun was rising up among the stars
That rose with him when the Divine Love

First set those lovely things in motion,
So I was encouraged to face with better hope
The beast skipping in its merry skin

By the time of day, the sweetness of the season:
But not enough not to be frightened by
The sudden apparition of a lion

That came for me with his head in the air
And so maddened by hunger it seemed
The air itself was bristling with fear.

And a she-wolf, so thin she looked as if
All her appetites were gnawing at her.
She had already brought many to grief

And I was so scared at the sight of her
My courage broke and I lost heart
In climbing the mountain any farther.

And like somebody keyed up to win
Who, when the time comes round for him to lose,
Weeps, and is inconsolably cast down—

I was like that as I retreated from
The animal's turbulent head-on attack
Gradually, to where the sun is dumb.

While I was slipping back, about to sink
Back to the depths, I caught sight of one
Who seemed through a long silence indistinct.

When I saw him in that great waste land
I cried out to him, 'Pity me,
Whatever you are, shade or living man.'

He answered, 'No, I am not a living man
Though I was alive once, and had Lombards
For parents, both of them Mantuan.

Though I was born *sub Julio*, my prime
Was spent in the heyday of the false gods
When I lived in Rome, in good Augustus's time.

I was a poet, and I sang of that just son
Of Anchises who came out of Troy
After the burning of proud Illion.

But why do you face back into misery?
Why do you not keep on up the sweet hill,
The source and cause of all felicity?'

'O are you then Virgil, are you the fountainhead
Of that wide river of speech constantly brimming?'
I answered and for shame kept my head bowed.

'All other poets live by your honour and light.
Let me be enabled by the great love
That impelled me to your book and bound me to it.

You are my master, my authority.
I learned from you and from you alone
The illustrious style for which they honour me.

Look at the beast that has forced me to turn back.
O help me to confront her, famous sage,
For she makes my veins race and my pulses shake.'

'You will have to go another way around,'
He answered, when he saw me weeping,
'To escape the toils and thickets of this ground;

Because this animal you are troubled by
Lets no man pass but harasses him
Until she kills him by her savagery

And she is so consumed by viciousness
That nothing fills her, and so insatiable
That feeding only makes her ravenous.

There are many animals she couples with
And there will be more of them, until the Hound
Shall come and grind her in the jaws of death.

He will not feed on money or on earth,
But wisdom, virtue and love will sustain him
And between two bits of felt he will have his birth.

To humble Italy, for which the virgin
Camilla died bleeding, and Turnus died, and Nisus
And Euryalus, he will bring salvation.

He will hunt the wolf through every town
Until he has hounded her down to hell
Where envy first unleashed her and set her on.

Therefore, for your own good, I think the best course
Is to follow me and I will be your guide
And lead you from here through an eternal place

Where you will hear hopeless screams and see
The long-lost spirits suffering their pain,
Lamenting the second death they have to die.

And then you will see those who are not distressed
In the fire because they hope to come,
Whenever their time comes, among the blessed.

If you want to ascend among these, then you
Will be guided by a soul worthier than I
And I will leave you with her when I go;

For that Emperor above does not allow
Entry to me into His city
Because I was a rebel to His law.

His empire is everywhere but His high seat
And city are there, in His proper kingdom.
O happy is the man He calls to it.'

And I said to him, 'I ask you, poet,
In the name of that God you were ignorant of—
To prevent worse happening, to help me flee it—

Lead me to that place described by you
So that I may see St. Peter's Gate
And those other ones you spoke of in their sorrow.'

Then he set off and I began to follow.
                              Dante, Inferno, *Canto I.*

Michael Longley

b. 1939

WREATHS

The Civil Servant

He was preparing an Ulster fry for breakfast
When someone walked into the kitchen and shot him:
A bullet entered his mouth and pierced his skull,
The books he had read, the music he could play.

He lay in his dressing gown and pyjamas
While they dusted the dresser for fingerprints
And then shuffled backwards across the garden
With notebooks, cameras and measuring tapes.

They rolled him up like a red carpet and left
Only a bullet hole in the cutlery drawer:
Later his widow took a hammer and chisel
And removed the black keys from his piano.

The Greengrocer

He ran a good shop, and he died
Serving even the death-dealers
Who found him busy as usual
Behind the counter, organised
With holly wreaths for Christmas,
Fir trees on the pavement outside.

Astrologers or three wise men
Who may shortly be setting out
For a small house up the Shankill
Or the Falls, should pause on their way

To buy gifts at Jim Gibson's shop,
Dates and chestnuts and tangerines.

The Linen Workers

Christ's teeth ascended with him into heaven:
Through a cavity in one of his molars
The wind whistles: he is fastened for ever
By his exposed canines to a wintry sky.

I am blinded by the blaze of that smile
And by the memory of my father's false teeth
Brimming in their tumbler: they wore bubbles
And, outside of his body, a deadly grin.

When they massacred the ten linen workers
There fell on the road beside them spectacles,
Wallets, small change, and a set of dentures:
Blood, food particles, the bread, the wine.

Before I can bury my father once again
I must polish the spectacles, balance them
Upon his nose, fill his pockets with money
And into his dead mouth slip the set of teeth.

PEACE
after Tibullus

Who was responsible for the very first arms deal—
The man of iron who thought of marketing the sword?
Or did he intend us to use it against wild animals
Rather than ourselves? Even if he's not guilty
Murder got into the bloodstream as gene or virus
So that now we give birth to wars, short cuts to death.
Blame the affluent society: no killings when

The cup on the dinner table was made of beechwood,
And no barricades or ghettos when the shepherd
Snoozed among sheep that weren't even thoroughbreds.

I would like to have been alive in the good old days
Before the horrors of modern warfare and warcries
Stepping up my pulse rate. Alas, as things turn out
I've been press-ganged into service, and for all I know
Someone's polishing a spear with my number on it.
God of my Fathers, look after me like a child!
And don't be embarrassed by this handmade statue
Carved out of bog oak by my great-great-grandfather
Before the mass-production of religious art
When a wooden god stood simply in a narrow shrine.

A man could worship there with bunches of early grapes,
A wreath of whiskery wheat-ears, and then say Thank you
With a wholemeal loaf delivered by him in person,
His daughter carrying the unbroken honeycomb.
If the good Lord keeps me out of the firing line
I'll pick a porker from the steamy sty and dress
In my Sunday best, a country cousin's sacrifice.
Someone else can slaughter enemy commanders
And, over a drink, rehearse with me his memoirs,
Mapping the camp in wine upon the table top.

It's crazy to beg black death to join the ranks
Who dogs our footsteps anyhow with silent feet—
No cornfields in Hell, nor cultivated vineyards,
Only yapping Cerberus and the unattractive
Oarsman of the Styx: there an anaemic crew
Sleepwalks with smoky hair and empty eye-sockets.
How much nicer to have a family and let
Lazy old age catch up on you in your retirement,
You keeping track of the sheep, your son of the lambs,
While the woman of the house puts on the kettle.

I want to live until the white hairs shine above
A pensioner's memories of better days. Meanwhile
I would like peace to be my partner on the farm,
Peace personified: oxen under the curved yoke;
Compost for the vines, grape-juice turning into wine,
Vintage years handed down from father to son;
Hoe and ploughshare gleaming, while in some dark corner
Rust keeps the soldier's grisly weapons in their place;
The labourer steering his wife and children home
In a hay cart from the fields, a trifle sozzled.

Then, if there are skirmishes, guerilla tactics,
It's only lovers quarrelling, the bedroom door
Wrenched off its hinges, a woman in hysterics,
Hair torn out, cheeks swollen with bruises and tears—
Until the bully-boy starts snivelling as well
In a pang of conscience for his battered wife:
Then sexual neurosis works them up again
And the row escalates into a war of words.
He's hard as nails, made of sticks and stones, the chap
Who beats his girlfriend up. A crime against nature.

Enough, surely, to rip from her skin the flimsiest
Of negligees, ruffle that elaborate hair-do,
Enough to be the involuntary cause of tears—
Though upsetting a sensitive girl when you sulk
Is a peculiar satisfaction. But punch-ups,
Physical violence, are out: you might as well
Pack your kit-bag, goose-step a thousand miles away
From the female sex. As for me, I want a woman
To come and fondle my ears of wheat and let apples
Overflow between her breasts. I shall call her Peace.

THE WEST

Beneath a gas-mantle that the moths bombard,
Light that powders at a touch, dusty wings,
I listen for news through the atmospherics,
A crackle of sea-wrack, spinning driftwood,
Waves like distant traffic, news from home,

Or watch myself, as through a sandy lens,
Materialising out of the heat-shimmers
And finding my way for ever along
The path to this cottage, its windows,
Walls, sun and moon dials, home from home.

IN MEMORY OF GERARD DILLON

I

You walked, all of a sudden, through
The rickety gate which opens
To a scatter of curlews,
An acre of watery light; your grave
A dip in the dunes where sand mislays
The sound of the sea, earth over you
Like a low Irish sky; the sun
An electric light bulb clouded
By the sandy tides, sunlight lost
And found, a message in a bottle.

II

You are a room full of self-portraits,
A face that follows us everywhere;
An ear to the ground listening for
Dead brothers in layers; an eye
Taking in the beautiful predators—

Cats on the windowsill, birds of prey
And, between the diminutive fields,
A dragonfly, wings full of light
Where the road narrows to the last farm.

III

Christening robes, communion dresses,
The shawls of factory workers,
A blind drawn on the Lower Falls.

ON SLIEVE GULLION
for Douglas Carson

On Slieve Gullion 'men and mountain meet',
O'Hanlon's territory, the rapparee,
Home of gods, backdrop for a cattle raid,
The Lake of Cailleach Beara at the top
That slaked the severed head of Conor Mor:

To the south the Border and Ravensdale
Where the torturers of Nairac left
Not even an eyelash under the leaves
Or a touch for MacCecht the cupbearer
To rinse, then wonder where the water went.

I watch now through a gap in the hazels
A blackened face, the disembodied head
Of a mummer who has lost his bearings
Or, from the garrison at Dromintee,
A paratrooper on reconnaisance.

He draws a helicopter after him,
His beret far below, a wine-red spot
Swallowed by heathery patches and ling

As he sweats up the slopes of Slieve Gullion
With forty pounds of history on his back.

Both strangers here, we pass in silence
For he and I have dried the lakes and streams
And Conor said too long ago: 'Noble
And valiant is MacCecht the cupbearer
Who brings water that a king may drink.'

Seamus Deane

b. 1940

HISTORY LESSONS
for Ronan Sheehan and Richard Kearney

'The proud and beautiful city of Moscow
Is no more.' So wrote Napoleon to the Czar.
It was a November morning when we came
On this. I remember the football pitches
Beyond, stretched into wrinkles by the frost.
Someone was running across them, late for school,
His clothes scattered open by the wind.

Outside Moscow we had seen
A Napoleonic, then a Hitlerian dream
Aborted. The firegold city was burning
In the Kremlin domes, a sabred Wehrmacht
Lay opened to the bone, churches were ashen
Until heretics restored their colour
And their stone. Still that boy was running.

Fragrance of Christ, as in the whitethorn
Brightening through Lent, the stricken aroma
Of the Czars in ambered silence near Pavlovsk,
The smoking gold of icons at Zagorsk,
And this coal-smoke in the sunlight
Stealing over frost, houses huddled up in
Droves, deep drifts of lost

People. This was history, although the State
Exam confined Ireland to Grattan and allowed
Us roam from London to Moscow. I brought
Black gladioli bulbs from Samarkand
To flourish like omens in our cooler air;

Coals ripening in a light white as vodka.
Elections, hunger-strikes and shots

Greeted our return. Houses broke open
In the season's heat and the bulbs
Burned in the ground. Men on ladders
Climbed into roselight, a roof was a swarm of fireflies
At dusk. The city is no more. The lesson's learned.
I will remember it always as a burning
In the heart of winter and a boy running.

Derry, 1981

GUERILLAS

When the Portuguese came in
From manoeuvres in the North
Atlantic, they brought a scent
Of oranges and dark tobacco
To our Arctic streets. Norwegians,
However, were tall and cold,
Drinkers of cheap wine
That blued their eyes more
Than was good for anyone
Who bothered them. Some women
Became sailors' dolls and others
Disapproved. We smelt corruption
In the hot grease of liquor
And foreign language that spat
Around us in *The Moonlight Club.*
Some pleasure writhed there
And some fear. A fight occurred
And then there came the Military
Police who hammered silence out
With night sticks, wall to wall.
And then we'd steal the drinks

Left on the tables they had pushed
Aside to clear the floor.
The whiskey was watered, we could tell.
A medical treacle had been served
As rum. But that was business.
Pollution entered everything and made it
Fierce. Real life was so impure
We savoured its poisons as forbidden
Fruit and, desolate with knowledge,
Grew beyond redemption. Teachers
Washed their hands of us.
Innocent of any specific crime,
We were beaten for a general guilt,
Regular as clockwork. We watched
And questioned nothing. There would be a time
When the foreign sailors would be gone.
Business would still be business.
Whiskey would still be watered,
Some girls would still be dolls;
The Arctic would have inched nearer,
Pollution have gone deeper
And life, entirely domestic, would carry on.

OSIP MANDELSTAM

'The people need poetry.' That voice
That was last heard asking for warm
Clothes and money, also knew the hunger
We all have for the gold light
The goldfinch carries into the air
Like a tang of crushed almonds.

Nine months before heart-failure
Silenced his silk-sharp whistle
That haunted the steppes as though

A small shrapnel of birds scattered,
Bukharin, his protector, was shot
Along with Yagoda, Rykov, others.

The kerosene flash of his music
Leaps from the black earth,
From the whitening dead of the War
Who burn in its flammable spirit.
The fire-crop smokes in the Kremlin's
Eyes and the scorched marl

Cinders. Son of Petropolis, tell us,
Tell us how to turn into the flash,
To lie in the lice-red shirt
On the bank of the Styx and wait
For the gossamer of Paradise
To spider in our dirt-filled eyes.

READING PARADISE LOST
IN PROTESTANT ULSTER

Should I give in to sleep? This fire's warm,
I know the story off by heart,
Was up so late last night and all the harm
That can be done is done. Far apart
From Milton's devils is the present crew
Of zombie soldiers and their spies,
Supergrasses in whose hiss
We hear the snake and sense the mist
Rise in dreams that crowd the new
Awaking with their demobbed cries.

In the old ground of apocalypse
I saw a broken church near where
Two lines of trees came to eclipse

The summer light. Beside the stair
A grey crow from an old estate
Gripped on the book of Common Prayer,
A rope of mice hung on a strip
Of altar-cloth and a blurring date
Smeared the stone beneath the choir.

Awake again, I see the window take
An arc of rainbow and a fusing rain.
None should break the union of this State
Which God with Man conspired to ordain.
But the woe the long evening brings
To the mazy ambushes of streets
Marks us more deeply now than that bower
Of deepest Eden in our first parents' hour
Of sexual bliss and frail enamourings
Could ever do. Our "sovran Planter" beats

Upon his breast, dyadic evil rules;
A syncope that stammers in our guns,
That forms and then reforms itself in schools
And in our daughters' couplings and our sons'.
We feel the fire's heat, Belial's doze;
A maiden city's burning on the plain;
Rebels surround us, Lord. Ah, whence arose
This dark damnation, this hot unrainbowed rain?

Michael Hartnett

b. 1941

from THE PURGE

Hartnett, the poet, might as well be dead,
enmeshed in symbol—the fly in the web;
and November dribbles through the groves
and metaphors descend on him in droves:
the blood-sucked symbols—the sky so blue,
the lark, the kiss, and the rainbow too.
This syrupy drivel would make you puke.

The monarch now of an inch of vision,
I'll not fall down for indecision
but banish for now and forever after
the rusty hinges, the rotten rafters,
the symbols, the cant, the high allusion
that reduce the white mind to confusion.
Inspiration comes, and the poet is left
with the empty rattle of discarded shells,
the husks of beetles piled up dead—
his poem spoiled by stupid talk
that sucks the blood of an ancient craft
like a bloated tick on a mongrel's balls.
I must purge my thought and flay my diction
or else suffer that fierce affliction—
my poems only wind and bombast
having lost their human language.

Pleasant the young poet's dance with books
but the old poet's advance should be rebuffed—
the mummer in the tinker's shawl,
the garrulous brass-thief, the jackdaw,
the beat-up chair at the carpenter's,
and the scabby mouths of idle whores.

Bad cess to him who first compared
the poet's rhymes to the singing bird—
he insulted plumage, he insulted verse.
May Egypt shit him from a swallow's arse.
The fledgling's sweet, but it's insipid
to hear the chaffinch act the meadow-pipit.
Look at all our native birds
in stinking cages dung-floored,
their nests, the cast-offs of the age
where the birds moult in frightful rage.
They court and welcome the louse of fame
and, dying old, they die in vain:
ignorant, with nothing left,
but dregs and leavings. Outside the nest
the dance is stopped, the din consigned
to empty souls, to vacant minds.

My uncle's ribs are clattering
in my pocket. And hear again—
on the stairs the cacophony
of granny's skull (this symphony
of bones)—Priests' and Brothers' cries—
the wounded soul in my father's eyes:
the coarse whisper of my youth.
My ancestors march in dark pursuit:
Uncle Hate and Auntie Guilt,
I adore you both and your ancient quilts:
a poet must be true to his sources.
He wears a necklace of his mother's teeth;
with his brother's skin, his book's bound neat;
he's a curer of skins, a burier of corpses.
An eternal penance, this opening of graves—
the poets in the graveyards always with spades
and shovels fighting over bones—
one shines his sister's kneecap's dome,
one scrapes maggots from his mother's womb.
Each poem in elegy, a litany, or lament;

each line morbid with the hideous dead;
and hung around each poet's neck
are the tanned relics of his father's scrotum. . . .

Zeus and Venus, fables from the Hedge-
schools, fill us and take the edge
from thirst and poem-hunger: we're now well fed
and the University listens to our belch.
Mars with his shield incites, amused,
when the land of old soldiers is badly ruled
and aflame with discontented youth.
Goodbye to frippery, to jewellery, the toy;
to Jove and Gráinne and Daedalus, goodbye;
to Churches hung with miracles
like sheeps' afterbirth by Holy Wells.

A poet must master words, must learn his trade;
must be schooled in poetry, know how poems are made:
every poem in the world, its song and make.
Avoid labels and lepers' bells,
avoid the pedant pedagogical:
no poet is without colour, without stone, without chord.
But colour and granite won't yield to words,
the impoverished poet's syllables.
The poet's fugues add wind to wind
and wreck the work of greater men,
but white and empty, day and night,
we dose ourselves with others' thought
and stumble blithely to the heap of husks
and carouse safely in the pub—
we're no bees replete in the hive
but drunken wasps in the height of horrors
from sucking too much vinegar.

And always at night, antique Tradition,
lizard-infested, screams its mission:
"assonance! alliteration!" and "free verse!"

its retinue of poets shove up its arse
their ancient airs and metaphors. . . .

I am the grave of hope and the tomb of truth,
swiller of fame, gulper of residues.
The systems of great men will never mend
my heart's drop-down, the leak of sentiment.
I construct myself with Plato's ears,
Hegel's thumb, Freud's beard,
Nietzsche's 'tache and Bergson's teeth
to make my body whole, complete.
I add Buddha to the crush
and Lao Tzu's teachings are a must:
but a pain in my belly upsets my powers
and my body explodes in a rain of flowers,
and down I come with a shower of poets—
oh, they're some flowers, these perfumed oafs
with juniper of Aristotle, bogcotton of Kant,
sage of Schopenhauer, arrogant.
Here in a wood among stem and branch
like a child lost at a hurling match,
I hear the cheering of lusty throats
and see only the hems of coats.
Oh, I am Frankenstein and his creature
made of spittle, and bits and pieces. . . .

Imagine a world with nothing but poems,
desert-naked and bare-boned:
with nothing but swans and lilies and roses—
such a meagre fauna and flora.
All the foliage in technicolour,
dwarf and giant, joy and squalor.
If poets celebrate the world's soul
and the rare and wonderful they extol,
where's the mention of the plover?
Where's the nest of the water-dipper?
If no bird sang but Philomel,

and nothing was but sunrise, sunset,
the world we live in would be hell.
We're the boys who adore freedom
wanting only the praise of people:
we're the boys who fatten geese
to swell their livers for our feast.
We lost the election for our party,
the rags we wear make tailors narky.
We promise you silk and we give you cotton,
we fill the world with wrens from top to bottom.

The poet is only his Collected Verse,
and all he was is contained in books:
his poetry is his true memorial—
other than that, mere fables and stories.
Our viaticum is knowledge
and death wants nothing from us
but ourselves and our knowledge.
The brave man spends knowledge freely
Or else grows frightened, growing lonely;
and the straws fall that he stole from others—
his roof leaks on him. He shudders:
his bloated soul no more will hunger
and his once white mind is white no longer
and the thatch hardens, and the lights are smothered.
To die without knowledge of yourself
is the worst darkness, the worst hell:
to bequeath your truth to humanity
is the only immortality.
A jackdaw's death is a death, without question—
a nest torn down by the storms of autumn.

Statement is castrated verse—
a cry, a slogan—so we've heard:
the hymn of the pompous clerk.
Once our country was Róisín Dubh:
today it's a warlord, a stoat with a hood,

a sandy beach with an oil-soaked bird.
Of slogans now you can take your pick—
not poems or songs but rhetoric.
Where verse is treacherous, 'tis fitting and right
for the poet to turn fighter with an armalite!
A poem in prison isn't worth a fart—
won't dent a helmet, won't stop a shot:
won't feed a soul when the harvest rots,
won't put food in hungry pots.
Famine and war to all historians!
May popstars roar our ballads glorious!
Justice is the poet's land:
he has no family but a load
of dreams to sting, and coax, and goad
with words as worthless as tin cans.
May heavy boots stomp on the head
that forgets the danger of being understood. . . .

Butter my hand with reputation,
spread the terrible jam of my friends' ruination.
'Tis seldom you see a poet honest:
he strokes the foal that praises his sonnets—
that brute would bite—keep your hands far from it.
The tribe, the people, and the race
are rightly blamed, and rightly praised;
but there's no friend in that spooky parlour—
just sheets like shrouds over tables, over spectres.
A poet can fill his life
with family, friends, his kids, the wife,
but none can answer his overwhelming question:
how poets exist with no attention.
Loner or gregarious, sane or mad,
worn from nourishing the cuckoo in his head
expert in envy, lord of the absurd,
attracting every jibe and snigger in the world:
strewing pride and presents among the crowds
beside the grotesque tables and the shrouds,

in the parlour of his head mourning and weeping—
homeless, friendless, among his people.

Poetry is a rat trapped: it cannot live
in the fangs of allusion, the fangs of adjective,
poisonous both, especially the latter,
sweet as the Munster thrushes' chatter,
their songs like goat-shit on a drum.
The adjective produces a sickly noun,
and all my rhymes are maternity homes
where nouns are patients and mothers both,
and my Lord Adjective is outside
waiting his chance of another ride.
Cut 'em down, and dry, and turn 'em,
and make a heap of 'em and burn 'em
and through the smoke, our names you'll see:
no tree is green—a tree is a tree.
A tree is a name, and real too:
green is only a point of view.
But be careful when the scythe swings
for the stubble is full of warshocked limbs.
Give poetry a hand, undo its collar,
give the noun air, or it will smother.

A critic floundered in a poem once
for want of signposts, the poor dunce.
He crushed each sublety underfoot
and wept, hearing their brittle crunch.
He prayed to God that he might see,
he invoked the ghosts of the University.
"Straight ahead", came the blessed answer,
"to line twenty-nine, and look for Dante",
and released, he praised the poem, the chancer.
He saw no polish, or craft, or care,
nor the subtle power of the poet aware—
only that ugly signpost there.
His compass was of no account

in a place that had no north or south.
What's a critic, in the name of Bridget,
or can any "objective correlative" gauge it?
So, what is left when the piper ceases?
Dregs, spit, echoes and treacle.

There's still a problem, all said and done:
the poem that lives, will it be human?
I break my dictum—it's not a rule
but a harness on me, poetry's mule.

I am a conspiracy of one.
I'm humble, arrogant; all said and done,
my rules are easily broken:
I fill ten books to say: let nothing be spoken.
Serve the eclipse, keep a slice of the moon,
be a small light, be an exception too.
Suck the plum, spit out the stone—
it will land on dung
and a thousand trees will grow.
Don't be competitive: all we have is poems,
things not answerable
to leader and pope.

This is Ireland, and I'm myself,
I preach the gospel of non-assent.
Love and art is the work I want
as empty as a dipper's nest,
whiter than a goose's breast—
the poet's road with no milestone on it,
a road with no wayside stop upon it,
a road of insignificant herbs
welling quietly from every hedge.

a translation by Gabriel Fitzmaurice
of AN PHURGÓID

A VISIT TO CASTLETOWN HOUSE
for Nora Graham

The avenue was green and long, and green
light pooled under the fernheads; a jade screen
could not let such liquid light in, a sea
at its greenest self could not pretend to be
so emerald. Men had made this landscape
from a mere secreting wood: knuckles bled
and bones broke to make this awning drape
a fitting silk upon its owner's head.

The house was lifted by two pillared wings
out of its bulk of solid chisellings
and flashed across the chestnut-marshalled lawn
a few lit windows on a bullock bawn.
The one-way windows of the empty rooms
reflected meadows, now the haunt
of waterbirds: where hawtrees were in bloom,
and belladonna, a poisonous plant.

A newer gentry in their quaint attire
looked at maps depicting alien shire
and city, town and fort: they were his seed,
that native who had taken coloured beads
disguised as chandeliers of vulgar glass
and made a room to suit a tasteless man
—a graceful art come to a sorry pass—
painted like some demented tinker's van.

But the music that was played in there—
that had grace, a nervous grace laid bare,
Tortellier unravelling sonatas
pummelling the instrument that has
the deep luxurious sensual sound,
allowing it no richness, making stars

where moons would be, choosing to expound
music as passionate as guitars.

I went into the calmer, gentler hall
in the wineglassed, chattering interval:
there was the smell of rose and woodsmoke there.
I stepped into the gentler evening air
and saw black figures dancing on the lawn,
Eviction, Droit de Seigneur, Broken Bones:
and heard the crack of ligaments being torn
and smelled the clinging blood upon the stones.

Eamon Grennan

b. 1941

LIZARDS IN SARDINIA

I miss our lizards. The one who watched us
lunch on the rocks, half of him
sandstone brown, the other half neat rings
of neon avocado. He moved his head in
wary jerks, like a small bird. Unblinking,
his stillness turned him stone. When he
shifted, whiptail, his whole length flowed
like water. Those reptile eyes of his
took in a world we couldn't see, as he
paused in the dragon-roar of sunlight till
his blood boiled again, then lit out for shadows
and an age of fragrance. The other one
who'd lost his tail and stumped about, still
quick as a lizard, vanishing behind the trunk
of the eucalyptus. Two who scuttled circles,
tail of one clamped fast in the other's
mouth: courtship, you hoped, as they dervished
among the piebald, finger-slim, fallen leaves
and rustled into infinity—a flash,
an absence—minute leftovers with molten brains,
escapees when their sky-high brothers bowed
cloud-scraping heads and bit the dust, leaving
the wrecked armadas of their ribs
for us to wonder at. Or that plump one
squatting beside me at the edge of the steel
and turquoise bay you rose from dripping light
and smiling in my direction: unblemished emerald
down half his length, the rest opaque and
dull, we thought, until we saw the envelope
of old skin he was shedding, under which

jewel-bright he blazed our breath away, like
the one I dreamt when my father died, big
as an iguana and the colour of greaseproof paper
till I saw him gleam and be a newborn beast of
jade and flame who stood there mildly casting
his old self off and shining. Those afternoons
after we'd made love I lay quite still
along your back, blood simmering, and saw
your splayed palms flatten on the white sheet
like a lizard's, while we listened, barely
breathing, to the wind whiffle the eucalyptus
leaves against the window, our new world
steadying around us, its weather settled.

INCIDENT
for Louis Asekoff

Mid-October, Massachusetts. We drive
through the livid innards of a beast, dragon
or salamander, whose home is fire. The hills
a witch's quilt of goldrust, flushed cinnamon,
wine fever, hectic lemon. After dark, while
water ruffles, salted, in the big pot, we four
gather towards the woodfire, exchanging
lazy sentences, waiting dinner. Sunk
in the supermarket cardboard box
the four lobsters tip and coolly stroke each other
with rockblue baton legs and tentative
antennae, their breath a wet clicking, the undulant
slow shift of their plated bodies
like the doped drift of patients
in the padded ward. Eyes like squished berries
out on stalks. It's the end of the line
for them, yet faintly in that close-companioned air

they smell the sea, a shadow-haunted hole to hide in
till all this blows over.

When it's time,
we turn the music up to nerve us
to it, then take them one by one and drop
in the salty roil and scald, then clamp
the big lid back. Grasping the shapely fantail
I plunge mine in headfirst and feel
before I can detach myself the flat slap
of a jackknifed back, glimpse for an instant
before I put the lid on it
the rigid backward bow-bend of the whole body
as the brain explodes and lidless eyes
sear white. We two are bound in silence
till the pot-lid planks back and music
floods again, like a tide. Minutes later
the four of us bend to brittle pink intricate
shells, drawing white sweet flesh
with our fingers, sewing our shroud-talk
tight about us. Later, near moonless midnight,
when I scrape the leafbright broken remains
into the garbage-can outside, that last
knowing spasm eels up my arm again
and off, like a flash, across the rueful stars.

SOUL MUSIC: THE DERRY AIR

A strong drink, hundred-year-old
schnapps, to be sipped at, invading
the secret places that lie in wait
and lonely between bone and muscle, or
counting (Morse code for insomniacs)
the seconds round the heart
when it stutters to itself. Or to be

taken in at the eyes in small doses,
phrase by somatic phrase, a line
of laundry after dawn, air clean as
vodka, snow all over, the laundry
lightly shaking itself
from frigid sleep. Shirts, flowered sheets,
pyjamas, empty trousers, empty
socks—risen as at a last day's dawn
to pure body, light as air. Whiteness
whiter than snow, blueness bluer than
new day brightening the sky-lid
behind trees stripped of their illusions
down to a webbed geometry
subtler than speech. A fierce blue eye
farther off than God, witnessing
house-boxes huddled together
for comfort, fronting blindly
the deserted streets down which in time
come farting lorries full of soldiers.
You are a fugitive *I*, a singing
nerve: you flit from garden to garden
in your fit of silence, bits of you
flaking off in steam and sizzling
like hot fat in the snow. Listen
to the pickers and stealers, the shots,
man-shouts, women wailing, the cry of kids
who clutch stuffed dolls or teddy bears
and shiver, gripping tight as a kite
whatever hand is offered. Here
is the light glinting on top-boots, on
the barrel of an M-16 that grins, holding
its breath, beyond argument. And here is
a small room where robust winter sunlight
rummages much of the day when the day
is cloudless, making some ordinary potted plants
flower to your surprise again, again,

and again: pink, anemic red, wax-white
their resurrection petals. Like hearts
drawn by children, like oiled arrowheads,
their unquestioning green leaves seem
alive with expectation.

Derek Mahon

b. 1941

A DISUSED SHED IN CO. WEXFORD

Let them not forget us, the weak souls among the asphodels.
    —SEFERIS, *Mythistorema*

for J. G. Farrell

Even now there are places where a thought might grow—
Peruvian mines, worked out and abandoned
To a slow clock of condensation,
An echo trapped for ever, and a flutter
Of wildflowers in the lift-shaft,
Indian compounds where the wind dances
And a door bangs with diminished confidence,
Lime crevices behind rippling rainbarrels,
Dog corners for bone burials;
And in a disused shed in Co. Wexford,

Deep in the grounds of a burnt-out hotel,
Among the bathtubs and the washbasins
A thousand mushrooms crowd to a keyhole.
This is the one star in their firmament
Or frames a star within a star.
What should they do there but desire?
So many days beyond the rhododendrons
With the world waltzing in its bowl of cloud,
They have learnt patience and silence
Listening to the rooks querulous in the high wood.

They have been waiting for us in a foetor
Of vegetable sweat since civil war days,
Since the gravel-crunching, interminable departure
Of the expropriated mycologist.

He never came back, and light since then
Is a keyhole rusting gently after rain.
Spiders have spun, flies dusted to mildew
And once a day, perhaps, they have heard something—
A trickle of masonry, a shout from the blue
Or a lorry changing gear at the end of the lane.

There have been deaths, the pale flesh flaking
Into the earth that nourished it;
And nightmares, born of these and the grim
Dominion of stale air and rank moisture.
Those nearest the door grow strong—
'Elbow room! Elbow room!'
The rest, dim in a twilight of crumbling
Utensils and broken flower-pots, groaning
For their deliverance, have been so long
Expectant that there is left only the posture.

A half century, without visitors, in the dark—
Poor preparation for the cracking lock
And creak of hinges. Magi, moonmen,
Powdery prisoners of the old regime,
Web-throated, stalked like triffids, racked by drought
And insomnia, only the ghost of a scream
At the flash-bulb firing squad we wake them with
Shows there is life yet in their feverish forms.
Grown beyond nature now, soft food for worms,
They lift frail heads in gravity and good faith.

They are begging us, you see, in their wordless way,
To do something, to speak on their behalf
Or at least not to close the door again.
Lost people of Treblinka and Pompeii!
'Save us, save us,' they seem to say,
'Let the god not abandon us
Who have come so far in darkness and in pain.
We too had our lives to live.

You with your light meter and relaxed itinerary,
Let not our naive labours have been in vain!'

THE GLOBE IN NORTH CAROLINA

'There are no religions, no revelations; there are women.'
—VOZNESENSKY, *Antiworlds*

The earth spins to my finger-tips and
Pauses beneath my outstretched hand;
White water seethes against the green
Capes where the continents begin.
Warm breezes move the pines and stir
The hot dust of the piedmont where
Night glides inland from town to town.
I love to see that sun go down.

It sets in a coniferous haze
Beyond Tennessee; the Anglepoise
Rears like a moon to shed its savage
Radiance on the desolate page,
On Dvořák sleeves and Audubon
Bird-prints. An electronic brain
Records the concrete music of
Our hardware in the heavens above.

From Hatteras to the Blue Ridge
Night spreads like ink on the unhedged
Tobacco fields and clucking lakes,
Bringing the lights on in the rocks
And swamps, the farms and motor courts,
Substantial cities, kitsch resorts—
Until, to the mild theoptic eye,
America is its own night-sky,

Its own celestial fruit, on which
Sidereal forms appear, their rich
Clusters and vague attenuations
Miming galactic dispositions.
Hesperus is a lighthouse, Mars
An air-force base; molecular cars
Arrowing the turnpikes become
Lost meteorites in search of home.

No doubt we could go on like this
For decades yet; but nemesis
Awaits our furious make-believe,
Our harsh refusal to conceive
A world so different from our own
We wouldn't know it were we shown.
Who, in its halcyon days, imagined
Carthage a ballroom for the wind?

And what will the new night be like?
Why, as before, a partial dark
Stage-lit by a mysterious glow
As in the *Night Hunt* of Uccello.
Era-provincial self-regard
Finds us, as ever, unprepared
For the odd shifts of emphasis
Time regularly throws up to us.

Here, as elsewhere, I recognize
A wood invisible for its trees
Where everything must change except
The fact of change; our scepticism
And irony, grown trite, be dumb
Before the new thing that must come
Out of the scrunched Budweiser can
To make us sadder, wiser men.

Out in the void and staring hard
At the dim stone where we were reared,
Great mother, now the gods have gone
We put our faith in you alone,
Inverting the procedures which
Knelt us to things beyond our reach.
Drop of the oceans, may your salt
Astringency redeem our fault!

Veined marble, if we only knew,
In practice as in theory, true
Salvation lies not in the thrust
Of action only, but the trust
We place in our peripheral
Night garden in the glory-hole
Of space, a home from home, and what
Devotion we can bring to it!

...You lie, an ocean to the east,
Your limbs composed, your mind at rest,
Asleep in a sunrise which will be
Your mid-day when it reaches me;
And what misgivings I might have
About the true importance of
The merely human pale before
The mere fact of your being there.

Five miles away a south-bound freight
Shrieks its euphoria to the state
And passes on; unfinished work
Awaits me in the scented dark.
The halved globe, slowly turning, hugs
Its silence, and the lightning bugs
Are quiet beneath the open window
Listening to that lonesome whistle blow ...

ST. EUSTACE

The hunt ceases
Here: there will be no more
Deranged pursuit of the mild-eyed
Creatures of the countryside.
Startled. he reins before
His nemesis

And stares amazed
At the hanged man of wood—
Gawain caught in the cold cathedral
Light of a temperate forest, Paul
Blind on a desert road,
One hand upraised.

He will not burn,
Now, with such nonchalance
Agape beasts to the gods of Rome
Whose strident, bronze imperium
He served devoutly once
But in his turn

Rotate above
A charcoal brazier,
Braised in his own fat for his contumacy
And vision; in his dying briefly
One with the hind, the hare
And the ring-dove.

ACHILL

im chaonaí uaigneach nach mór go bhfeicim an lá

I lie and imagine a first light gleam in the bay
    After one more night of erosion and nearer the grave,
Then stand and gaze from a window at break of day
    As a shearwater skims the ridge of an incoming wave;
And I think of my son a dolphin in the Aegean,
    A sprite among sails knife-bright in a seasonal wind,
And wish he were here where currachs walk on the ocean
    To ease with his talk the solitude locked in my mind.

I sit on a stone after lunch and consider the glow
    Of the sun through mist, a pearl bulb containedly fierce;
A rain-shower darkens the schist for a minute or so
    Then it drifts away and the sloe-black patches disperse.
Croagh Patrick towers like Naxos over the water
    And I think of my daughter at work on her difficult art
And wish she were with me now between thrush and plover,
    Wild thyme and sea-thrift, to lift the weight from my
        heart.

The young sit smoking and laughing on the bridge at
        evening
    Like birds on a telephone pole or notes on a score.
A tin whistle squeals in the parlour, once more it is raining,
    Turfsmoke inclines and a wind whines under the door;
And I lie and imagine the lights going on in the harbour
    Of white-housed Náousa, your clear definition at night,
And wish you were here to upstage my disconsolate labour
    As I glance through a few thin pages and switch off the
        light.

KINSALE

The kind of rain we knew is a thing of the past,
deep-delving, dark, deliberate you would say,
browsing on spire and bogland; but today
our sky-blue slates are steaming in the sun,
our yachts tinkling and dancing in the bay
like racehorses. We contemplate at last
shining windows. a future forbidden to no-one.

DEATH AND THE SUN
(Albert Camus, 1913–1960)

Le soleil ni la mort ne se peuvent regarder fixement.
—LA ROCHEFOUCAULD

When the car spun from the road and your neck broke
I was hearing rain on the school bicycle shed
Or tracing the squeaky enumerations of chalk;
And later, while you lay in the *mairie*,
I pedaled home from Bab-el-Oued
To my mother silently making tea,
Bent to my homework in the firelight
Or watched an old film on television—
Gunfights under a blinding desert sun,
Bogartian urgencies in the Ulster night.

How we read you then, admiring the frank composure
Of a stranger bayed by dogs who could not hear
The interior dialogue of flesh and stone,
His life and death a work of art
Conceived in the silence of the heart.
Not that he would ever have said so, no,
He would merely have taken a rush-hour tram
To a hot beach white as a scream,

Stripped to a figure of skin and bone
And struck out, a back-stroke, as far as he could go.

Deprived though we were of his climatic privileges
And raised in a northern land of rain and murk,
We too knew the familiar foe, the blaze
Of headlights on a coast road, the cicadas
Chattering like watches in our sodden hedges;
Yet never imagined the plague to come,
So long had it crouched there in the dark—
The *cordon sanitaire*, the stricken home,
Rats on the pavement. rats in the mind,
'St. James Infirmary' playing to the plague wind.

'An edifying abundance of funeral parlours',
The dead on holiday, cloth caps and curlers,
The shoe-shine and the thrice-combed wave
On Sunday morning and Saturday night;
Wee shadows fighting in a smoky cave
Who would one day be brought to light—
The modes of pain and pleasure,
These were the things to treasure
When times changed and your kind broke camp.
Diogenes in the dog-house, you carried a paraffin lamp.

Meanwhile in the night of Europe, the winter of faces,
Sex and opinion. a deft hand removes
The Just Judges from their rightful places
And hangs them behind a bar in Amsterdam—
A desert of fog and water. a cloudy dream
Where an antique Indonesian god grimaces
And relativity dawns like a host of doves;
Where the goalie who refused suicide
Trades solidarity for solitude,
A night watch, a self-portrait, supper at Emmaus.

The lights are going on in towns that no longer exist.
Night falls on Belfast, on the just and the unjust,
On its Augustinian austerities of sand and stone—
While Sisyphus' descendants, briefly content,
Stand in the dole queues and roll their own.
Malraux described these preterite to you
As no longer historically significant;
And certainly they are shrouded in white dust.
All souls leprous, blinded by truth, each ghost
Steams on the shore as if awaiting rescue.

One cannot stare for long at death or the sun.
Imagine Plato's neolithic troglodyte
Released from his dark cinema, released even
From the fire proper, so that he stands at last,
Absurd and anxious, out in the open air
And gazes, shading his eyes, at the world there—
Tangible fact ablaze in a clear light
That casts no shadow, where the vast
Sun gongs its lenity from a brazen heaven
Listening in silence to his rich despair.

A POSTCARD FROM BERLIN
(for Paul Durcan)

We know the cities by their stones
Where Ararat flood-water shines
And violets have struggled through
The bloody dust. Skies are the blue
Of postcard skies, and the leaves green
In that quaint quarter of Berlin.
Wool-gatheringly, the clouds migrate:
No checkpoint checks their tenuous flight.

I hear echoes of Weimar tunes,
Grosz laughter in the beer-gardens
Of a razed Reich, and rumbling tyres
Unter den Linden; but the fires
Of abstract rage, exhausted there,
Blaze out of control elsewhere—
Perhaps one reason you pursue
This night-hunt with no end in view.

I can imagine your dismay
As, cornered in some zinc café,
You read of another hunger-strike,
A postman blasted off his bike . . .
Oh, Hölderlin no fly would hurt,
Our vagabond and pilgrim spirit,
Give us a ring on your way back
And tell us what the nations lack!

John F. Deane

b. 1943

ON A DARK NIGHT

On a dark night
When all the street was hushed, you crept
Out of our bed and down the carpeted stair.
I stirred, unknowing that some light
Within you had gone out, and still I slept.
As if, out of the dark air

Of night, some call
Drew you, you moved in the silent street
Where cars were white in frost. Beyond the gate
You were your shadow on a garage-wall.
Mud on our laneway touched your naked feet.
The dying elms of our estate.

Became your bower
And on your neck the chilling airs
Moved freely. I was not there when you kept
Such a hopeless tryst. At this most silent hour
You walked distracted with your heavy cares
On a dark night while I slept.

Paul Durcan

b. 1944

THE HAT FACTORY

Eleven o'clock and the bar is empty
Except for myself and an old man;
We sit with our backs to the street-window,
The sun in the east streaming through it;
And I think of childhood and swimming
Underwater by a famine pier;
The ashlar coursing of the stonework
Like the bar-room shelves
Seen through tidal amber seaweed
In the antique mirror;
Now myself and the old man floating
In the glow of the early morning sun
Twined round each other and our newspapers;
And our pint glasses like capstans on the pier.
We do not read our daily charters
—Charters of liberty to know what's going on—
But hold them as capes before reality's bull
And with grace of ease we make our passes;
El Cordobes might envy this old small man
For the sweet veronicas he makes in daily life.
He is the recipient of an old age pension
While I am so low in society's scale
I do not rate even the dole
But I am at peace with myself and so is he;
Although I do not know what he is thinking
His small round fragile noble mouth
Has the look of the door of Aladdin's cave
Quivering in expectation of the magic word;
Open sesame;
I suspect that like me he is thinking

Of the nothing-in-particular;
Myself, I am thinking of the local hat factory,
Of its history and the eerie fact
That in my small town I have never known
Anyone who worked in it
Or had to be with it at all;
As a child I used to look through a hole in the hedge
At the hat factory down below in the valley;
I used to lie flat on my face in the long grass
And put out my head through the hole;
Had the hatters looked out through their porthole windows
They would have seen high up in the hillside
A long wild hedgerow broken only
By the head of the child looking out through the hole;
I speculate;
And as to what kind of hats they make;
And do they have a range in black birettas;
And do they have a conveyor belt of toppers;
And do the workers get free hats?
And I recall the pope's skull-cap
Placed on my head when as a boy-child
In a city hospital I lay near to death
And the black homburg of the red-nosed undertaker
And the balaclavas of assassins
And the pixies of the lost children of the murdered earth;
And the multi-coloured yamulka of the wandering Jew
And the black kippa of my American friend
In Jerusalem in the snow
And the portly Egyptian's tiny fez
And the tragic Bedouin's kefia in the sands of sun
And the monk's cowl and the nun's wimple
And the funereal mortarboards of airborn puritans
And the megalithic coifs of the pan-cake women of Brittany
And the sleek fedoras of well-to-do thugs
And sadistic squires' napoleonic tricorns
And prancing horse-cavalry in their cruel shakos
And the heroic lifeboatman's black sou'wester

And the nicotine-stained wig of the curly-haired barrister
And the black busby used as a handbag by my laughing
    brother
And the silken turban of the highbrow widow
And foreign legionaries in nullah kepis
And Mayday praesidiums in astrakhans
And bonnets and boaters and sombreros and stetsons
And stove-pipes and steeples and mantillas and berets
And topis and sun-hats and deer-stalkers and pill-boxes
And naughty grandmothers in toques
And bishops' mitres and soldier's helmets;
And in Languedoc and in Aran—cloth caps.
And what if you were a hatter
And you married a hatter
And all your sons and daughters worked as hatters
And you inhabited a hat-house all full of hats:
Hats, hats, hats, hats:
Hats: the apotheosis of an ancient craft
And I think of all the nationalities of Israel
And of how each always clings to his native hat,
His priceless and moveable roof,
His hat which is the last and first symbol
Of a man's slender foothold on this earth.
Women and girls also work in the factory
But not many of them wear hats;
Some wear scarves, but rarely hats;
Now there'll be no more courting of maidens
In schooner hats on dangerous cliffs;
It seems part of the slavery of liberation
To empty relationships of all courtship
Of which hats were an exciting part.
Probably, I shall never wear a hat:
So thus I ask the old man
If I may look at his trilby
—Old honesty—
And graciously he hands it to me
And with surprise

I note that it was manufactured
In the local hat factory
And I hand it back to him
—A crown to its king—
And like a king he blesses me when he goes
Wishing me a good day before he starts
His frail progress home along the streets,
Along the lanes and terraces of the hillside,
To his one up and one down.
I turn about and see
Over the windowpane's frosted hemisphere
A small black hat sails slowly past my eyes
Into the unknown ocean of the sun at noon.

IRISH HIERARCHY BANS COLOUR PHOTOGRAPHY

After a Spring meeting in their nineteenth century fastness at
    Maynooth
The Irish Hierarchy has issued a total ban on the practice of
    colour photography:
A spokesman added that while in accordance with tradition
No logical explanation would be provided
There were a number of illogical explanations which he would
    discuss;
He stated that it was not true that the ban was the result
Of the Hierarchy's tacit endorsement of racial discrimination;
(And, here, the spokesman, Fr. Marksman, smiled to himself
But when asked to elaborate on his smile, he would not
    elaborate
Except to growl some categorical expletives which included
    the word 'liberal')
He stated that if the Press corps would countenance an
    unhappy pun
He would say that negative thinking lay at the root of the ban;
Colour pictures produced in the minds of people,

Especially in the minds (if any) of young people,
A serious distortion of reality;
Colour pictures showed reality to be rich and various
Whereas reality in point of fact was the opposite;
The innate black and white nature of reality would have to be
    safeguarded
At all costs and, talking of costs, said Fr Marksman,
It ought to be borne in mind, as indeed the Hierarchy had
    borne in its collective mind,
That colour photography was far costlier than black and white
    photography
And, as a consequence, more immoral;
The Hierarchy, stated Fr Marksman, was once again smiting
    two birds with one boulder;
And the joint-hegemony of Morality and Economics was being
    upheld.

The total ban came as a total surprise to the accumulated
    Press corps
And Irish Roman Catholic pressmen and presswomen present
Had to be helped away as they wept copiously in their cups:
"No more oranges and lemons in Maynooth" sobbed one
    cameraboy.
The general public, however, is expected to pay no heed to
    the ban;
Only politicians and time-servers are likely to pay the required
    lip-service;
But the operative noun is lip: there will be no hand or foot
    service.
And next year Ireland is expected to become
The E.E.C.'s largest money-spender in colour photographer:

This is Claudia Conway RTE News (Colour) Maynooth.

THE JEWISH BRIDE
(after Rembrandt)

At the black canvas of estrangement,
As the smoke empties from the ruins under a gold Winter sky,
Death-trains clattering across the back gardens of Amsterdam
—Sheds, buckets, wire, concrete
—Manholes, pumps, pliers, scaffolding:
I see, as if for the first time,
The person you were, and are, and always will be
Despite the evil that men do:
The teenage girl on the brink of womanhood
Who, when I met you, was on the brink of everything—
Composing fairytales and making drawings
That used to remind your friends of Anderson and Thurber—
Living your hidden life that promised everything
Despite all the maimed, unreliable men and women
Who were at that moment congregating all around you:
Including, of course, most of all, myself.
You made of your bedroom a flowing stream
Into which, daily, you threw proofs of your dreams;
Pinned to your bedroom wall with brass-studded drawing pins
Newspaper and magazine photographs of your heroes and
     heroines,
People who met you breathed the air of freedom,
And sensuality fragile as it was wild:
'Nessa's air makes free' people used to say,
Like in the dark ages, 'Town air makes free'.
The miracle is that you survived me.
You stroll about the malls and alleyways of Amsterdam,
About its islands and bridges, its archways and jetties,
With Spring in your heels, although it is Winter;
Privately, publicly, along the Grand Parade;
A Jewish Bride who has survived the death-camp,
Free at last of my swastika eyes
Staring at you from across spiked dinner plates
Or from out of the bunker of a TV armchair;

Free of the glare off my jackboot silence;
Free of the hysteria of my gestapo voice;
Now your shyness replenished with all your old cheeky
confidence—
That grassy well at which red horses used to rear up and sip
With young men naked riding bareback calling your name.
Dog-muzzle of tension torn down from your face;
Black polythene of asphyxiation peeled away from your soul;
Your green eyes quivering with dark, sunny laughter
And—all spread-eagled and supple again—your loving,
freckled hands.

AROUND THE CORNER FROM FRANCIS BACON

Around the corner from Francis Bacon
Was where we made our first nest together
On the waters of the flood;
Where we first lived in sin:
The sunniest, most virtuous days of our life.
Not even the pastoral squalor of Clapham Common
Nor the ghetto life of Notting Hill Gate
Nor the racial drama of Barcelona
Nor the cliffhanging bourgeois life of Cork City
Could ever equal those initial, primeval times together
Living in sin
In the halcyon ambience of South Kensington,
A haven for peaceful revolutionaries such as Harriet Waugh
Or Francis Bacon, or ourselves.
I slept on an ironing board in the kitchen
And you slept in the attic:
Late at night when all the other flat-dwellers
Were abed and—we thought wishfully—asleep,
You crept down the attic ladder
To make love with me on the ironing board,

As if we had known each other in a previous life
So waterily did our two body-phones attune,
Underwater swimming face to face in the dark,
Francis Bacon-Cimabue style.
My body-phone was made in Dublin
But your body-phone was made in Japan.
Standing up naked on the kitchen floor,
In the smog-filtered moonlight,
You placed your hand on my little folly, murmuring:
I have come to iron you, Sir Board.
Far from the tyrant liberties of Dublin, Ireland,
Where the comedy of freedom was by law forbidden
And truth, since the freedom of the state, gone
        underground.
When you had finished ironing me
I felt like hot silk queueing up to be bathed
Under a waterfall in Samarkand
Or a mountain stream in Enniskerry.
Every evening I waited for you to come home,
Nipping out only in the rush hour to the delicatessen,
Where Francis Bacon, basket under arm,
Surfacing like Mr. Mole from his mews around the corner,
Used to be stocking up in tomato purée and curry powder
Before heading off into the night and 'The Colony Room
        Club'
Into whose green dark you and I sometimes also tip-toed.
In your own way you were equally Beatrix Potter-like,
Coming home to me laden with fish fingers and baked
        beans.
While I read to you from Dahlberg, you tuaght me about
        the psyche
Of the female orang-outang caged in the zoo:
Coronation Street ... Z Cars ... The World in Action ...
Then Z Cars to beat all Z Cars—our own world in action—
The baskets of your eyes chock-a-block with your unique
        brands

Of tomato purée and curry powder;
Or, *That Was The Week That Was*, and then, my sleeping
    friend,
In the sandhills of whose shoulders sloping secretly down
Into small, hot havens of pure unscathèd sands
Where the only sounds are the sounds of the sea's tidal waters
Flooding backwards and forwards,
Tonight is the night that always is forever—
Ten or twenty minutes in the dark,
And in four million years or so
My stomach will swarm again suddenly with butterflies,
As with your bowl of water and your towel,
Your candle and your attic ladder,
Your taut high wire and your balancing pole,
A green mini-dress over your arm, a Penguin paperback in
    your hand,
I watch you coming towards me in the twilight of rush hour
On your hands and knees
And on the wet, mauve tip of your extended tongue
The two multi-coloured birds of your plumed eyes ablaze
Around the corner from Francis Bacon.

10:30 AM MASS, JUNE 16, 1985

When the priest made his entrance on the altar on the stroke
    of 10:30
He looked like a film star at an international airport
After having flown in from the other side of the world,
As if the other side of the world was the other side of the
    street;
Only, instead of an overnight bag slung over his shoulder,
He was carrying the chalice in its triangular green veil—
The way a dapper comedian cloaks a dove in a silk
    handkerchief.
Having kissed the altar, he strode over to the microphone:

I'd like to say how glad I am to be here with you this
    morning.

Oddly, you could see quite well that he was genuinely glad—
As if, in fact, he had been actually looking forward to this
    Sunday service,
Much the way I had been looking forward to it myself;
As if, in fact, this was the big moment of his day—of his
    week,
Not merely another ritual to be sanctimoniously performed.
He was a small, stocky, handsome man in his forties
With a big mop of curly grey hair
And black, horn-rimmed, tinted spectacles.
I am sure that more than half the women in the church
Fell in love with him on the spot—
Not to mention the men.
Myself, I felt like a cuddle.
The reading from the prophet Ezekiel (17:22–24)
Was a lot of old codswallop about cedar trees in Israel
(It's a long way from a tin of steak-and-kidney pie
For Sunday lunch in a Dublin bedsit
To cedar trees in Israel),
And the epistle was even worse—
St. Paul on his high horse and, as nearly always,
Putting his hoof in it—prating about 'the law court of Christ'
(Director of Public Prosecutions, Mr. J. Christ, Messiah)!
With the Gospel, however, things began to look up—
The parable of the mustard seed as being the kingdom of
    heaven;
Now then the Homily, at best probably inoffensively boring.

It's Father's Day—this small, solid, serious, sexy priest began—
And I want to tell you about my own father
Because none of you knew him.
If there was one thing he liked, it was a pint of Guinness;
If there was one thing he liked more than a pint of Guinness
It was two pints of Guinness.

But then when he was fifty-five he gave up drink.
I never knew why, but I had my suspicions.
Long after he had died my mother told me why:
He was so proud of me when I entered the seminary
That he gave up drinking as his way of thanking God.
But he himself never said a word about it to me—
He kept his secret to the end. He died from cancer
A few weeks before I was ordained a priest.
I'd like to go to Confession—he said to me:
OK—I'll go and get a priest—I said to him:
No—don't do that—I'd prefer to talk to you:
Dying, he confessed to me the story of his life.
How many of you here at Mass today are fathers?
I want all of you who are fathers to stand up.

Not one male in transept or aisle or nave stood up—
It was as if all the fathers in the church had been caught out
In the profanity of their sanctity,
In the bodily nakedness of their fatherhood,
In the carnal deed of their fathering;
Then, in ones and twos and threes, fifty or sixty of us
          clambered to our feet
And blushed to the roots of our being.
Now—declared the priest—let the rest of us
Praise these men our fathers.
He began to clap hands.
Gradually the congregation began to clap hands,
Until the entire church was ablaze with clapping hands—
Wives vying with daughters, sons with sons,
Clapping clapping clapping clapping clapping,
While I stood there in a trance, tears streaming down my
          cheeks:
Jesus!
I want to tell you about my own father
Because none of you knew him!

THE DIVORCE REFERENDUM, IRELAND 1986

By the time the priest started into his sermon
I was adrift on a leaf of tranquillity,
Feeling only the need and desire to praise,
To feed praise to the tiger of life.
Hosanna Hosanna Hosanna.
He was a gentle-voiced, middle-aged man
Slightly stooped under a gulf of grey hair,
Slightly tormented by an excess of humility.
He talked felicitously of the Holy Spirit—
As if he really believed in what he was preaching
—Not as if he was aiming to annotate a diagram
Or to sub-edit the gospel—
But as if the Holy Spirit was as real as rainwater.
Then, all of a sudden, his voice changed colour—
You could see it change from pink into white—
And he remarked icily: "It is the wish of the Hierarchy
That today the Clergy of Ireland put before you
Christ's teaching on the indissolubility of marriage
And to remind you that when you vote in the Divorce
    Referendum
The Church's teaching and Christ's teaching are one and the
    same."
Stunned, I stared up at him from my pew
As he stood there supported by candles and gladioli,
Vestments, and altarboys at his feet;
I could feel my breastplate tighten and my shoulderblades
    quiver
And I knew the anger that Jesus Christ felt
When he drove from the temple the traders and stockbrokers:
I have come into this temple today to pray
And be healed by, and joined with, the Spirit of Life;
Not to be invaded by politics and ideology.
I say unto you, preacher, and orators of the Hierarchy,
Do not bring politics and ideology into my house of prayer.

I closed my eyes
And I did not open them again until I could hear
The priest murmuring the prayers of the Consecration.
At Holy Communion I kept my eyes on a small girl
To whom the priest had to bend low to give her the host.
Curtseying, she smiled eagerly, and flew back down the aisle
Carrying in her breast the Eucharist of her innocence:
May she have children of her own
And as many husbands as will praise her
For what are husbands for, but to praise their wives?

Eavan Boland

b. 1945

WOMAN IN KITCHEN

Breakfast over, islanded by noise,
She watches the machines go fast and slow.
She stands among them as they shake the house.
They move; their destination is specific.
She has nowhere definite to go.
She might be a pedestrian in traffic.

White surfaces retract; white
Sideboards light the white of walls.
Cups wink white in their saucers.
The light of day bleaches as it falls
On cups and sideboards. She could use
The room to tap with if she lost her sight.

Machines jigsaw everything she knows
And she is everywhere among their furor:
The tropic of the dryer tumbling clothes,
The round lunar window of the washer.
The kettle in the toaster is a kingfisher
Roving for trout above the river's mirror.

The wash done, the kettle boiled, the sheets
Spun and clean, the dryer stops dead.
The silence is a death: it starts to bury
The room in white spaces. She turns to spread
A cloth on the board and irons sheets
In a room white and quiet as a mortuary.

THE BLACK LACE FAN MY MOTHER GAVE ME

It was the first gift he ever gave her,
buying it for five francs in the Galeries
in prewar Paris. It was stifling.
A starless drought made the nights stormy.

They stayed in the city for the summer.
They met in cafés. She was always early.
He was late. That evening he was later.
They wrapped the fan. He looked at his watch.

She looked down the Boulevard des Capucines.
She ordered more coffee. She stood up.
The streets were emptying. The heat was killing.
She thought the distance smelled of rain and lightning.

These are wild roses, appliquéd in silk
by hand—darkly picked, stitched boldly, quickly.
The rest is tortoiseshell and has the reticent,
clear patience of its element. It is

a worn-out, underwater bullion and it keeps,
even now, an inference of its violation.
The lace is overcast, as if the weather
it opened for and offset had entered it.

The past is an empty café terrace.
An airless dusk before thunder. A man running.
And no way now to know what happened then—
none at all—unless, of course, you improvise:

The blackbird on this first sultry morning
in summer, finding buds, worms, fruit,
feels the heat. Suddenly, she puts out her wing—
the whole, full, flirtatious span of it.

THE JOURNEY

And then the dark fell and 'there has never,'
I said, 'been a poem to an antibiotic:
never a word to compare with the odes on
the flower of the raw sloe for fever

'or the devious Africa-seeking tern
or the protein treasures of the sea bed.
Depend on it, somewhere a poet is wasting
his sweet uncluttered metres on the obvious

'emblem instead of the real thing.
Instead of sulpha we shall have hyssop dipped
in the wild blood of the unblemished lamb,
so every day the language gets less

'for the task and we are less with the language'.
I finished speaking and the anger faded
and dark fell and the book beside me
lay open at the page Aphrodite

comforts Sappho in her love's duress.
The poplars shifted their music in the garden,
a child startled in a dream.
my room was a mess—

the usual hardcovers, half-finished cups.
clothes piled up on an old chair—
and I was listening out but in my head was
a loosening and sweetening heaviness.

not sleep but nearly sleep, not dreaming really
but as ready to believe and still
unfevered, calm and unsurprised,
when she came and stood beside me

and I would have known her anywhere
and I would have gone with her anywhere
and she came wordlessly
and without a word I went with her

down down down without so much as
ever touching down but always, always
with a sense of mulch beneath us,
the way of stairs winding down to a river

and as we went on the light went on
failing and I looked sideways to be certain
it was she, misshapen, musical—
Sappho—the scholiast's nightingale,

and down we went, again down
until we came to a sudden rest
beside a river in what seemed to be
an oppressive suburb of the dawn.

My eyes got slowly used to the bad light.
At first I saw shadows, only shadows.
Then I could make out women and children
and, in the way they were, the grace of love.

'Cholera, typhus, croup, diptheria,'
she said. 'in those days they racketed
in every backstreet and alley of old Europe.
Behold the children of the plague.'

Then to my horror I could see to each
nipple some had clipped a limpet shape—
suckling darknesses—while others had their arms
weighed down, making terrible *pietàs*.

She took my sleeve and said to me, 'be careful.
Do not define these women by their work:

not as washerwomen trussed in dust and sweating,
muscling water into linen by the river's edge

'nor as court ladies brailled in silk
on wool and woven with an ivory unicorn
and hung, nor as laundresses tossing cotton,
brisking daylight with lavender and gossip.

'But these are women who went out like you
when dusk became a dark sweet with leaves,
recovering the day, stooping, picking up
teddy bears and rag dolls and tricycles and buckets—

love's archaeology—and they too like you
stood boot deep in flowers once in summer
or saw winter come in with a single magpie
in a caul of haws, a solo harlequin.'

I stood fixed. I could not reach or speak to them.
Between us was the melancholy river,
the dream water, the narcotic crossing,
and they had passed over it, its cold persuasions.

I whispered, 'let me be
let me at least be their witness,' but she said,
'what you have seen is beyond speech,
beyond song, only not beyond love;

'remember it, you will remember it,'
and I heard her say but she was fading fast
as we emerged under the stars of heaven,
'there are not many of us; you are dear

'and stand beside me as my own daughter.
I have brought you here so you will know forever
the silences in which are our beginnings,
in which we have an origin like water,'

and the wind shifted and the window clasp
opened, banged, and I woke up to find
the poetry books stacked higgledy piggledy,
my skirt spread out where I had laid it—

nothing was changed; nothing was more clear
but it was wet and the year was late.
The rain was grief in arrears; my children
slept the last dark out safely and I wept.

THE ACHILL WOMAN

She came up the hill carrying water.
She wore a half-buttoned wool cardigan,
a tea towel round her waist.

She pushed the hair out of her eyes with
her free hand and put the bucket down.

The zinc-music of the handle on the rim
tuned the evening. An Easter moon rose.
In the next-door field a stream was
a fluid sunset; and then, stars.

I remember the cold rosiness of her hands.
She bent down and blew on them like broth;
and, round her waist, on a white background
in coarse, woven letters the words "glass cloth."

She was nearly finished for the day.
And I was all talk, raw from College-
weekending at a friend's cottage
with one suitcase and the set text
of the court poets of the Silver Age.

We stayed putting down time until
the evening turned cold without warning.
She said goodnight and started down the hill.

The grass changed from lavender to black.
The trees turned back to cold outlines.
You could taste frost

but nothing now can change the way I went
indoors, chilled by the wind,
and made a fire
and took down my book
and opened it
and failed to comprehend

the harmonies of servitude,
the grace music gives to flattery
and language borrows from ambition

and how I fell asleep
oblivious to

the planets clouding over in the skies,
the slow decline of the spring moon,
the songs crying out their ironies.

Frank Ormsby

b. 1947

THE PADRE

We won't forget the padre in a hurry,
his big Norton pummelling the backroads.
He roars from among the laurels,
God's batman in oils and goggles,
or strides into pub brawls with sweet crosses,
calling for peace.

The padre has no special voice for prayer.
His talk is the right words for broken men
and village children,
Schulz in the sick-bay, anonymous with fear,
and little Goering, brooding on his name.

II

Meatpackers, truckers, longshoremen from Maine,
Slav lumberjacks, tough immigrants at home
on the wharves of the East River,
a Negro lad who lied about his age
in Jackson, Missouri.

On a wall outside the compound they have composed
their own exile's prayer, a dense litany
of half the towns in the Union:
Battle Creek, Michigan to Broken Bow,
Dripping Springs, Texas to Woodstock, Vermont.

My congregations.
All in uniform.
All in a strange country, passing through.

Ciarán Carson

b. 1948

CAMPAIGN

They had questioned him for hours. Who exactly was he? And
 when
He told them, they questioned him again. When they accepted
 who he was, as
Someone not involved, they pulled out his fingernails. Then
They took him to a waste-ground somewhere near the
 Horseshoe Bend, and told him
What he was. They shot him nine times.

A dark umbilicus of smoke was rising from a heap of burning
 tyres.
The bad smell he smelt was the smell of himself. Broken glass
 and knotted Durex.
The knuckles of a face in a nylon stocking. I used to see him
 in the Gladstone Bar,
Drawing pints for strangers, his almost-perfect fingers flecked
 with scum.

ARMY

The duck patrol is waddling down the odd-numbers side of
 Raglan Street,
The bass-ackwards private at the rear trying not to think of a
 third eye
Being drilled in the back of his head. Fifty-five. They stop.
 The head
Peers round, then leaps the gap of Balaclava Street. He waves
 the body over

One by one. Forty-nine. Cape Street. A gable wall. Garnet
    Street. A gable wall.

Frere Street. Forty-seven. Forty-five-and-a-half. Milan Street.
    A grocer's shop.
They stop. They check their guns. Thirteen. Milton Street. An
    iron lamp-post.
Number one. Ormond Street. *Two ducks in front of a duck and
    two ducks*
Behind a duck, how many ducks? Five? *No. Three.* This is not the
    end.

BELFAST CONFETTI

Suddenly as the riot squad moved in, it was raining
    exclamation marks,
Nuts, bolts, nails, car-keys. A fount of broken type. And the
    explosion
Itself—an asterisk on the map. This hyphenated line, a burst
    of rapid fire . . .
I was trying to complete a sentence in my head, but it kept
    stuttering,
All the alleyways and side-streets blocked with stops and
    colons.

I know this labyrinth so well—Balaclava, Raglan, Inkerman,
    Odessa Street—
Why can't I escape? Every move is punctuated. Crimea Street.
    Dead end again.
A Saracen, Kremlin-2 mesh. Makrolon face-shields. Walkie-
    talkies. What is
My name? Where am I coming from? Where am I going? A
    fusillade of question-marks.

COCKTAILS

Bombing at about ninety miles an hour with the exhaust
    skittering
The skid-marked pitted tarmac of Kennedy Way, they hit the
    ramp and sailed
Clean over the red-and-white guillotine of the check-point
    and landed
On the Ml flyover, then disappeared before the Brits knew
    what hit them. So
The story went: we were in the Whip and Saddle bar of the
    Europa.

There was talk of someone who was shot nine times and
        lived,
    and someone else
Had the inside info. on the Romper Room. We were trying to
    remember the facts
Behind the Black & Decker case, when someone ordered
    another drink and we entered
The realm of Jabberwocks and Angels' Wings, Widows'
    Kisses, Corpse Revivers.

Tom Paulin

b. 1949

STILL CENTURY

The hard captains of industry
Held the province in a firm control.

Judges, your pious tyranny
Is baked bone-dry in the old

Bricks of a hundred linen mills,
The shadows of black tabernacles.

A crowd moves along the Shankill,
And lamps shine in the dull

Streets where a fierce religion
Prays to the names of power:

Ewart and Bryson, Craig and Carson.
On every wall, texts or a thick char.

Stacked in the corners of factory-yards,
The wicker carboys of green acid

Hold out their bitter promise of whiteness
To the bleachgreens above the city.

The orange smoke at sunset, the gruff
Accents of a thousand foremen, speak

To the chosen, saying they are the stuff
The visions, cutlery and Belleek

China are laid on. They are tied
To the shade of a bearded god,

Their dream of happiness is his smile
And his skilful way with the hardest rod.

OF DIFFERENCE DOES IT MAKE

During the 51-year existence of the Northern Ireland Parliament only one Bill sponsored by a non-Unionist member was ever passed.

Among the plovers and the stonechats
protected by the Wild Birds Act
of nineteen-hundred-and-thirty-one,
there is a rare stint called the notawhit
that has a schisty flight-call, like the chough's.
Notawhit, notawhit, notawhit
—it raps out a sharp code-sign
like a mild and patient prisoner
pecking through granite with a teaspoon.

Medbh MacGuckian

b. 1950

LAURENTIA

The somnolence of star-stones, ice-tears,
Earth-fruit-light slows
In the unasked-for colours of diamonds.
On troubled islands difficult of access grows
The golden topaz maidenly as wine,
The wary turquoise, shot with cognac brown,
The satin sky-stone, its invigorating blue:

The anxious ruby darkens at the squatting pose
Of evil; beryls water-clear and sea-horse strewn,
Mull over the liquids in which they lie;
The virginal shimmering of moonstones
Awakens passion under the tongues
Of lovers till they will themselves
A downy street to the moon:

The modest tourmaline, as drowsy
As the solitary magnolia, draws ash
Out of a meerschaum pipe to speed
The flow of thought; and emeralds,
Casketed in locust-trees, never release
Their different pavilions,
Their Northern shield.

COLLUSION

The begonia's soil is rich and wet.
I tuck it in around her
As I would pat my hair,
Straightening her tubered root.

We keep our sources secret—she
Swells with lymph and electricity,
Her fibres transparently taped up, and I
Sprout willowy as any sweet begonia.

WATERFORD

The rich families ordered everything in crystal,
From covered urns to toddy-lifters;
The mushroom stoppers seldom sat
In the wide necks of their decanters,
The flaring lips of ewers—
The claret-jug was well-endowed
To meet the hard-drinking needs of the Irish
With its straight-sided, softly-shouldered profile.

The cutters snipped from furniture and dress
Their drapery swags and Van Dyke rims;
Their candlesticks were smooth as melted ice,
Or sharply silver-edged;
Handles were like swans' necks,
Dishes shaped in hearts, or leaves,
Vases for flower-roots; they had ears, or waists.
The tripod's legs a foot ending in toes.

Once in command of a colourless chastity,
The cutters naturally took it out on the surface,
Balancing impressions and depressions,

Filling the empty spaces with stars,
Or broad fields of strawberry diamonds.
Herringbone blazes and pillared flutes
Reflected the light on melon bowls,
Motifs on muffineers.

On plain glass everything was clearer—
The Williamite horse, 'Our True Deliverer',
The Volunteer toasting-glass, with cannon and shot,
The cordial-glasses boasting briefly
The short-lived symbols of the Union.
Hunting-vessels kept the shamrock and the hare,
The rich families sealed themselves
In roses and quills, laurel wreaths and crowns.

GATEPOSTS

A man will keep a horse for prestige,
But a woman ripens best underground.
He settles where the wind
Brings his whirling hat to rest,
And the wind decides which door is to be used.

Under the hip-roofed thatch,
The bed-wing is warmed by the chimney breast;
On either side the keeping-holes
For his belongings, hers.

He says it is unlucky to widen the house,
And leaves the gateposts holding up the fairies.
He lays his lazy-beds and burns the river,
He builds turf-castles, and sprigs the corn with apple-mint.

She spreads heather on the floor
And sifts the oatmeal ark for thin-bread farls:
All through the blue month
She tosses stones in basins to the sun,
And watches for the trout in the holy well.

Philip Casey

b. 1950

CASANOVA ON HIS DEATHBED

Darling Henriette, if fate were symmetrical,
you'd have made a happy mortal
of this dying wretch.
The disastrous façade that is suavity,
the calamity of manners which devour a man . . .
Henriette, did you for a moment see
the frightened child pride had blinded?

Or Pauline, queenly saint of Portugal,
whose love was the oblivion drug
I feared and craved.
My dearest, had you been free
to snatch me from the ghouls of freedom,
I'd be lying now, content,
eternal children circling their sire's bed.

There was but one offspring I know of,
one shimmering pearl from all the pearls I cast.
Sophie, Sophie my daughter, where are you now?
Child of my haughty years, where are you now?
Does my blood flow in blue, English veins?

I, dear child, am in the first circle of hell,
with not even the damned for company.

There was once an Irish miracle of beauty,
the one who scorned my version of the Iliad.
Perhaps Sarah, her eyes denying my existence,
could have saved me.
Or Hélène O-Morphi, the little Greek
I raised to fame, but who fell from grace.

I have driven bejewelled coaches across
the brilliant wasteland of my hedonist's quest,
across a thousand velvet bellies
which would not yield up their secret.
Finally naked,
I am poised at the mouth of the pit,
where wisdom is superfluous. I laugh
until the tears come, then laugh again.

Henriette, Pauline, Sarah, Sophie.
Lover, daughter, illusion
I cast my arms about you and fall deep
into a greedy darkness, finally whole.

Michael Davitt

b. 1950

IN MEMORY OF ELIZABETH KEARNEY, BLASKET-ISLANDER (†1974)

Once it was cards on the table,
Rosary and mugs of tea in candlelight
Beside a blazing fire;
Outside, a donkey in the night,
Dogs denied their diet
And an old woman destroying me with Irish.

Once, there was the after-Mass chatting,
And she would trim the sails
Of strangers with one caustic look of her eye
Putting the College Trippers
Firmly in their places
With 'pestles' and 'hencrabs' and 'haycocks'!

Once, at mackerel and potatoes
During the news at noon-time
She'd ask for a translation
Because her English was lacking
And I'd say: "Yera they're killing each other
In the North of Ireland."

Once, she was like a statue
At the top-stairs window
Wandering west from the quayside
Home in a dream to her island
And if I suddenly came up behind her
She'd say: "Oh, you thief, may you long be homeless!"

translated by the author

THE MIRROR
in memory of my father

I

He was no longer my father
but I was still his son;
I would get to grips with that cold paradox,
the remote figure in his Sunday best
who was buried the next day.

A great day for tears, snifters of sherry,
whiskey, beef sandwiches, tea.
An old mate of his was recounting
their day excursion
to Youghal in the Thirties,
how he was his first partner
on the Cork/Skibbereen route
in the late Forties.
There was a splay of Mass cards
on the sitting-room mantelpiece
which formed a crescent round a glass vase,
his retirement present from C.I.E.

II

I didn't realize till two days later
it was the mirror took his breath away.

The monstrous old Victorian mirror
with the ornate gilt frame
we had found in the three-storey house
when we moved in from the country.
I was afraid that it would sneak
down from the wall and swallow me up
in one gulp in the middle of the night.

While he was decorating the bedroom
he had taken down the mirror
without asking for help;
soon he turned the colour of terra-cotta
and his heart broke that night.

III

There was nothing for it
but to set about finishing the job,
papering over the cracks,
painting the high window,
stripping the door, like the door of a crypt.
When I took hold of the mirror
I had a fright. I imagined him breathing through it.
I heard him say in a reassuring whisper:
I'll give you a hand, here.

And we lifted the mirror back in position
above the fireplace,
my father holding it steady
while I drove home
the two nails.

translated by Paul Muldoon

Paul Muldoon

b. 1951

THE BEARDED WOMAN, BY RIBERA

I've seen one in a fairground,
Swigging a quart of whiskey,
But nothing like this lady
Who squats in the foreground
To suckle the baby,
With what must be her husband
Almost out of the picture.

Might this be the Holy Family
Gone wrong?

Her face belongs to my grand-da
Except that her beard
Is so luxuriantly black.
One pap, her right, is bared
And borrowed by her child,
Who could not be less childlike.
He's ninety, too, if he's a day.

I'm taken completely
By this so unlikely Madonna.

Yet my eye is drawn once again,
Almost against its wishes,
To the figure in the shadows,
Willowy, and clean-shaven,
As if he has simply wandered in
Between mending that fuse
And washing the breakfast dishes.

MEETING THE BRITISH

We met the British in the dead of winter.
The sky was lavender

and the snow lavender-blue.
I could hear, far below,

the sound of two streams coming together
(both were frozen over)

and, no less strange,
myself calling out in French

across that forest-
clearing. Neither General Jeffrey Amherst

nor Colonel Henry Bouquet
could stomach our willow-tobacco.

As for the unusual
scent when the Colonel shook out his hand-

kerchief: *C'est la lavande,*
une fleur mauve comme le ciel.

They gave us six fishhooks
and two blankets embroidered with smallpox.

THE SIGHTSEERS

My father and mother, my brother and sister
and I, with uncle Pat, our dour best-loved uncle,
had set out that Sunday afternoon in July
in his broken-down Ford

not to visit some graveyard—one died of shingles,
one of fever, another's knees turned to jelly—
but the brand-new roundabout at Ballygawley,
the first in mid-Ulster.

Uncle Pat was telling us how the B-Specials
had stopped him one night somewhere near Ballygawley
and smashed his bicycle

and made him sing the Sash and curse the Pope of Rome.
They held a pistol so hard against his forehead
there was still the mark of an O when he got home.

THE CENTAURS

I can think of William of Orange,
Prince of gasworks-wall and gable-end.
A plodding, snow-white charger
On the green, grassy slopes of the Boyne,
The milk-cart swimming against the current

Of our own backstreet. Hernán Cortez
Is mustering his cavalcade on the pavement,
Lifting his shield like the lid of a garbage-can.
His eyes are fixed on a river of Aztec silver.
He whinnies and paws the earth

For our amazement. And Saul of Tarsus,
The stone he picked up once has grown into a hoof.
He slings the saddle-bags over his haunches,
Lengthening his reins, loosening his girth.
To thunder down the long road to Damascus.

OUR LADY OF ARDBOE

I

Just there, in a corner of the whin-field,
Just where the thistles bloom.
She stood there as in Bethlehem
One night in nineteen fifty-three or four.

The girl leaning over the half-door
Saw the cattle kneel, and herself knelt.

II

I suppose that a farmer's youngest daughter
Might, as well as the next, unravel
The winding road to Christ's navel.

Who's to know what's knowable?
Milk from the Virgin Mother's breast,
A feather off the Holy Ghost?
The fairy thorn? The holy well?

Our simple wish for there being more to life
Than a job, a car, a house, a wife—
The fixity of running water.

For I like to think, as I step these acres,
That a holy well is no more shallow
Nor plummetless than the pools of Shiloh,
The fairy thorn no less true than the Cross.

III

Mother of our Creator, Mother of our Saviour,
Mother most amiable, Mother most admirable.
Virgin most prudent, Virgin most venerable,
Mother inviolate, Mother undefiled.

And I walk waist-deep among purples and golds
With one arm as long as the other.

GATHERING MUSHROOMS

The rain comes flapping through the yard
like a tablecloth that she hand-embroidered.
My mother has left it on the line.
It is sodden with rain.
The mushroom shed is windowless, wide,
its high-stacked wooden trays
hosed down with formaldehyde.
And my father has opened the Gates of Troy
to that first load of horse manure.
Barley straw. Gypsum. Dried blood. Ammonia.
Wagon after wagon
blusters in, a self-renewing gold-black dragon
we push to the back of the mind.
We have taken our pitchforks to the wind.

All brought back to me that September evening
fifteen years on. The pair of us
tripping through Barnett's fair demesne
like girls in long dresses
after a hail-storm.
We might have been thinking of the fire-bomb
that sent Malone House sky-high
and its priceless collection of linen
sky-high.
We might have wept with Elizabeth McCrum.
We were thinking only of psilocybin.
You sang of the maid you met on the dewy grass—

And she stooped so low gave me to know
it was mushrooms she was gathering O.

He'll be wearing that same old donkey-jacket
and the sawn-off waders.
He carries a knife, two punnets, a bucket.
He reaches far into his own shadow.
We'll have taken him unawares
and stand behind him, slightly to one side.
He is one of those ancient warriors
before the rising tide.
He'll glance back from under his peaked cap
without breaking rhythm:
his coaxing a mushroom—a flat or a cup—
the nick against his right thumb;
the bucket then, the punnet to left or right,
and so on and so forth till kingdom come.

We followed the overgrown tow-path by the Lagan.
The sunset would deepen through cinnamon
to aubergine,
the wood-pigeon's concerto for oboe and strings,
allegro, blowing your mind.
And you were suddenly out of my ken, hurtling
towards the ever-receding ground,
into the maw
of a shimmering green-gold dragon.
You discovered yourself in some outbuilding
with your long-lost companion, me,
though my head had grown into the head of a horse
that shook its dirty-fair mane
and spoke this verse:
Come back to us. However cold and raw, your feet
were always meant
to negotiate terms with bare cement.
Beyond this concrete wall is a wall of concrete
and barbed wire. Your only hope
is to come back. If sing you must, let your song
tell of treading your own dung,
let straw and dung give a spring to your step.

If we never live to see the day we leap
into our true domain,
lie down with us now and wrap
yourself in the soiled grey blanket of Irish rain
that will, one day, bleach itself white.
Lie down with us and wait.

Peter Fallon

b. 1951

MOONS

By the light of the harvest moon
the combine-harvester whose wheel
made of hill fields a Mississippi
paddled through the waving acres
to dock beside the shearing-shed.
We dried the grain and packed the barns,
stacked bales of oat- and barley-straw,
and McNamees let out the stubble geese.

By the light of the hunter's moon
as first frost fell and sloes bulged
like cows' eyes, the sounds of night
were sounds of foxes, nesting fowl,
reviving rivers, and we prepared.
We killed to eat or killed to purge
and I condemned the useless slaughter,
the gadgets used to draw the pelts.

I was driving home one night
and caught in my headlights a sundered pair
of badgers, a sow that moved, a boar
that didn't. She had lingered nearby
shuffling in bushes, quietly keening,
and nudged to remind the body be well.
Could she have travelled across
from the other world, this widow who scuffed

the beaten path through moonlight,
could she have come all these years on,
mumbling her music, her ancient warning?

I reached to touch the stiffening back
as after argument one would a lover
or as I reached to touch my father lying
late that morning turned towards the wall.
My shyness was fear, fear that he'd turn
on me again. I was afraid until I saw
the bruised blood stopped in his elbow.
I lay the badger in the ditch and looked
for her who trod both lights. She was nowhere
to be seen. She was leading me on,
leading me down the long halls of her sett,
bringing me back. A moon shone brightly
in front of me. There was home in its eclipse.

Gerald Dawe

b. 1952

THE LUNDYS LETTER

You staged the ultimate *coup de grâce*
for the Union's son turned republican.
I can see you shivering in the cold
of an East Belfast morning, outside
school, the bikes upended, the quad
blown by a dusty wind, and rows of
windows, some cellophaned, gaze
back at the encroaching estate.

Even your voice was different, haughty
we thought, the grand dismissive way
you demonstrated learning, or in *Tartuffe*
worked a subtle authority over our
ragged rebelliousness that we
should sit through such performances
of high art in a secondary school!

A generation growing but no hard-hats
for us or the miserable one-step up
a slippery ladder to civil service.
I don't know where you went; we got
lost in London or tried our wings
on an amalgam of desperate love
and politics at the new university.

And then the next time it was a warm
summer's day at Woolworth's when
the ground shook and a tailor's dummy
crashed through sheets of glass,
and there was hardly time to ask

how you were keeping as shoe-boxes flew
all over the place and the bomb
finished its work on down High Street.

Walking to the Dole, the clang in my ears
of sirens and trampling feet,
it was another lock of years
before I saw you in a pub by chance,
barely the same, chose not to recognise—
I only bear witness now to what was,
and hear you prefect's voice of derision
shout to a smoking third-form class.

Gerry Murphy

b. 1952

VISION AT KNOCK
(for Paul Durcan)

A figure,
perhaps John the Evangelist,
and behind John
an altar,
and on the altar,
a lamb,
and behind the lamb
a cross,
and behind the cross
a wet gable wall
and behind the wall
a poky interior,
and behind this poky interior
a dismal view of the countryside,
and beyond
this dismal view of the countryside
and a little to the right
the Cathedral of Minsk,
and behind
the Cathedral of Minsk
Stalin
laughing.

A SMALL FAT BOY WALKING BACKWARDS

I should have kept right on going
(smiling inwardly perhaps) and said

nothing until I was able to confide
in a policeman.
After all it could have been merely
a child's reaction to the probability
of imminent global destruction or to
the price of gold, or was it rumours
of a coup in Greece which troubled
his young socialist heart?

Anyway I couldn't resist inquiring
why he chose such an unorthodox
mode of conveyance with such grim
determination.
He told me to fuck off.

Yet consider if you will
the possibility that when
the Universe loses its tremendous
momentum of expansion and begins
to collapse back slowly on itself,
Time, Sex, Space, Previous Existence,
Tax Evasion, Syphilis, Early
Byzantium, Hitler and Coventry
Cathedral will reappear faster and
faster in final reverse order.

Harry Clifton

b. 1952

MONSOON GIRL

In the airconditioned drone
Of a room we rent by the hour,
You go to the telephone
Lovely and naked, to put through a call
For drinks, or hire a car
To take us home.

Your nudity dapples the walls
With shadows, and splashes the mirrors
Like a vision, in the blue light
That bathes you, a pleasure-girl
On a lost planet, sincere
But only at night.

Outside, it will rain
For weeks, months on end. . . .
We'll come here again
As we did before, where Chinese women,
Blank and inscrutable, attend
Nightly to our linen.

We'll come again
In drunkenness, for the child's play
Of lovemaking, or to part the rain
Like curtains of jet beads,
And dream the rainy months away
On pampered beds

Where forgetfulness lies down
With executive power

After hours, in a tangle of legs
And juices, a world turned upside down,
And I feed on the lotus-flower
Of your delicate sex.

At three, we'll be driven back
Through depths of Bangkok
Already tomorrow. There will be roads
Closed, and a dope squad
Flashing its query through windowglass,
Let us pass . . .

There will be lights
In Chinatown, sampans on the river—
The poor starting early. Elsewhere the night
Will separate us, having seeded within you
Miscarriage of justice forever,
And the rain will continue.

THE SEAMSTRESS

I have a seamstress, making a shirt for me
In sultry weather, in the months we are together.

She measures my shoulders with tape, I feel on my back
The cool of her wooden yardstick, and submit

To a temporary contract, binding me
To the new and the strange. Together we lose ourselves

Among shades of blue, the melancholy feast
A culture of silkworms creates, as Chinese tailors

Stand and wait. For me it's the stuff of dreams,
For her a labour of love . . . In her house on stilts

Where women are still slaves, she sews the collarless
Garment of pure freedom I have asked for

When I leave, keeping only for herself
Dry tailor's chalk, and the diagram of a body.

Nuala Ní Dhomhnaill

b. 1952

POEM FOR MELISSA

My fair-haired child dancing in the dunes
hair be-ribboned, gold rings on your fingers
to you, yet only five or six years old,
I grant you all on this delicate earth.

The fledgling bird out of the nest
the iris seeding in the drain
the green crab walking neatly sideways:
they are yours to see, my daughter.

The ox would gambol with the wolf
the child would play with the serpent
the lion would lie down with the lamb
in the pasture world I would delicately grant.

The garden gates forever wide open
no flaming swords in hands of Cherubim
no need for a fig-leaf apron here
in the pristine world I would delicately give.

Oh white daughter here's your mother's word:
I will put in your hand the sun and the moon
I will stand my body between the millstones
in God's mills so you are not totally ground.

VENIO EX ORIENTE

Eastern spices I bring with me,
and from bazaars, a mystery:

and perfumes from Arabic land
would not make bright your small white hand.

My hair is henna-brown
and pearls from my neck hang down
and my navel here conceals
vials of the honey of wild bees.

But my body breathes another musk
that smells of wild mint and turf:
scent of honey from an ancient hill
that has darkness in its tint.

I CANNOT LIE HERE ANYMORE ...

I cannot lie here anymore
in your aroma—
with your pillowed mouth
asnore,
your idle hand
across my hip
not really caring
whether I exist.

I'm not upset
because you ignore me
nor because our happy summer
washes over me—
it's not the bedside flowers
that intoxicate
but your body, your aroma,
a blend of blood and earth.

I'll get up from the bed
and put on my clothes

and leave with the carkeys
from your fist stolen
and drive to the city.

At nine tomorrow
you'll get a call
telling you where to go
to pick up your car—
but I cannot lie here anymore
where your aroma laps—
because I'll fall in love with you,
(perhaps)
translated by Michael Hartnett

THE BROKEN DOLL

O little broken doll, dropped in the well,
thrown aside by a child, scampering downhill
to hide under the skirts of his mother!
In twilight's quiet he took sudden fright
as toadstool caps snatched at his tongue,
foxgloves crooked their fingers at him
and from the oak, he heard the owl's low call.
His little heart almost stopped when a weasel
went by, with a fat young rabbit in its jaws,
loose guts spilling across the grass while
a bat wing flicked across the evening sky.

He rushed away so noisily and ever since
you are a lasting witness to the fairy arrow
that stabbed his ear; stuck in the mud
your plastic eyes squinny open from morning
to night: you see the vixen and her brood
stealing up to lap the ferny swamphole
near their sett, the badger loping to wash

his paws, snuff water with his snout. On
Pattern days people parade clockwise seven
rounds, at every turn, throw in a stone.

These small stones rain down on you.
The nuts from the hazel tree that grows
to the right of the well also drop down:
you will grow wiser than any blessed trout
in this ooze ! The red breasted robin
of the Sullivans will come to transform
the surface to honey with her quick tail,
churn the depths to blood, but you don't move.
Bemired, your neck strangled with lobelias,
I see your pallor staring starkly back at me
from every swimming hole, from every pool, Ophelia.
                              translated by John Montague

AS FOR THE QUINCE

There came this bright young thing
with a Black & Decker
and cut down my quince-tree.
I stood with my mouth hanging open
while one by one
she trimmed off the branches.

When my husband got home that
                              evening
and saw what had happened
he lost the rag,
as you might imagine.
'Why didn't you stop her?
What would she think
if I took the Black & Decker
round to her place

and cut down a quince-tree
belonging to her?
What would she make of that?'

Her ladyship came back next morning
while I was at breakfast.
She enquired about his reaction.
I told her straight
that he was wondering how she'd feel
if he took a Black & Decker
round to her house
and cut down a quince-tree of hers,
et cetera et cetera.

'O,' says she, 'that's very interesting.'
There was a stress on the 'very'.
She lingered over the 'ing.'
She was remarkably calm and collected.
These are the times that are in it, so,
all a bit topsy-turvy.
The bottom falling out of my belly
as if I had got a kick up the arse
or a punch in the kidneys.
A fainting-fit coming over me
that took the legs from under me
and left me so zonked
I could barely lift a finger
till Wednesday.

As for the quince, it was safe and
                                    sound
and still somehow holding its ground.
                    translated by Paul Muldoon

AUBADE

It's all the same to morning what it dawns on—
On the bickering of jackdaws in leafy trees;
On that dandy from the wetlands, the green mallard's
Stylish glissando among reeds; on the moorhen
Whose white petticoat flickers around the boghole;
On the oystercatcher on tiptoe at low tide.

It's all the same to the sun what it rises on—
On the windows in houses in Georgian squares;
On bees swarming to blitz suburban gardens;
On young couples yawning in unison before
They do it again; on dew like sweat or tears
On lilies and roses; on your bare shoulders.

But it isn't all the same to us that night-time
Runs out; that we must make do with today's
Happenings, and stoop and somehow glue together
The silly little shards of our lives, so that
Our children can drink water from broken bowls,
Not from cupped hands. It isn't the same at all.

translated by Michael Longley

Matthew Sweeney

b. 1952

A COUPLE WAITING

Leaving the door of the whitewashed house ajar
the man runs to the top of the hill
where he shields his eyes from the evening sun
and scans the sea. Behind him, a woman
holds a curtain back, but when he turns
and shakes his head, she lets the curtain fall.
She goes to the mirror beneath the flag
where she searches her face for signs of
the change her body tells her has begun.
The man shuts the door and sits at the table
where a chicken's bones are spread on two plates.
He thinks of his friends on the Atlantic,
coming up the western coast, laden
with well-wrapped bundles for his stable
that no horse uses. He thinks of his country,
and how his friends and he, with the help
of those bundles, would begin to set it right.
He calls the woman over and feels her stomach,
then asks why she thinks the boat is late.
Like him, she's harassed by an image—
the boat, searchlit, in French or Spanish waters,
guns pointed, a mouth at a megaphone.
Like him, she does not speak her mind,
instead sends him to the hill once more
in the dying light, to watch the red sun
sink in the water that's otherwise bare,
while she sits in the dark room, thinking
of the country their child will grow up in.

WHERE FISHERMEN CAN'T SWIM

Back there where fishermen can't swim,
where the ice-age coast of Donegal
leaves rocks among the waves,
a lobster-boat cast off, whose engine
croaked before the rocks were by.
The youngest in the crew leapt out
onto a rock to push the boat away,
then laughed when he couldn't jump back.
But exactly when did he realise
that the boat would float no nearer;
that all those pulls on the engine cord
would yield no shudders; that no rope
or lifebelt existed to be thrown;
that those flares were lost in cloud;
that the radio would bring a copter
an hour later? He had forty minutes—
to cling while the waves attacked,
to feel the rock gradually submerge.
And they had forty minutes of watching,
shouting into the radio, till he cried
out, sank from view, and stayed there.

Thomas Mc Carthy

b. 1954

THE SORROW GARDEN

I HOLE, SNOW

It is an image of irreversible loss,
This hole in my father's grave that needs
Continuous filling. Monthly now, my
Uncle comes to shovel a heap of earth
From the spare mound. Tear-filled, he
Compensates the collapse of his brother's
Frame. I arrive on my motor-bike to help
But he will not share the weight of grief.

It is six months since my father's death
And he has had to endure a deep snow;
All night it came down, silently like time,
Smoothing everything into sameness. I
Visited the winter-cold grave, expecting
A set of his footprints, a snow-miracle.

II SMALL BIRDS, VOICES

These are the neatly twisted sounds of death,
Those small brown birds singing, small winter
Birds clinging to an overhanging bough.
Never in life did I know him to stare
So silence-stricken for one brief moment.

These birds recall the voices of his life:
A low cold note is the voice of torment
From childhood poverty and the brief, light
Notes are the tones of Love and Marriage.

177

"There's the beginning of *your* life's troubles",
A neighbour said at his grave. I arranged
The wilting wreath-flowers, feigning numbness.
Something, perhaps his voice, told me even then
How much of love, sorrow, love one life contains.

III MISTING-OVER

These bright evenings I ride
through the young plantation
by the river; at times I can
see the young trees clearly
through the collapsing mist.

Sometimes in the misted river
at dusk his face at my left
shoulder has become distinctly
settled and lined with peace.

But now in the clouded pools
I drive through on the avenue,
he no longer calls out as if
injured by my rear wheel, but
is happy as clay, roads, memory.

IV LOST WORDS, SORROWS

It's difficult to believe that it could
go on; this wanting to participate
in a rigid plan of water and wood,
words and wood and other inanimate
worlds that cannot explain sorrow.

Around me I find the forms that know
his lack of living. The wooden sculpture
on a shelf points to its lack of finish,
calls for a finishing touch, for his sure
and solid polish. I pray for its wish.

As if water could explain my crying,
I visited the salmon-weir after
a snow-fall. The fish were maneuvering
through the spray, determined to get over
protective obstacles of wood and stone.

Like salmon through water, like virgin wood
disturbed into its form in art, his death
obfuscates words irrecoverably. Death plays
its own tune of vision and shadow. It has
attached itself as a vocabulary of change.

SHOPKEEPERS AT THE PARTY MEETING

Listen! Listen to shopkeepers talking
about the problems of land,
the breaking up of an estate
or a new acquisition.
Their conversation is
proprietorial. To talk
about a landlord's problem,
to articulate his burden,
is their act of possession.
They are owning the landscape,
briefly, with the magical
deeds of speech.

The Minister on the other hand
has no such words.
Whatever he has is secret,
even his desires. Especially his desires.
Shopkeepers move around the room,
excited, in debt,
spilling their dreams like salt.

PARTY SHRINE

Come back,
Poor Twenty-Sixer. Live on lack.
—AUSTIN CLARKE

My father is clearing the first Party shrine:
it is the summer of Sixty-Six.
He hates physical work and everything
that keeps him from the protection racket
of crosswords and history books.
But the rest of the Committee
has been drunk since the Jubilee
and can't break the spell of itself.

Weeds know nothing about the Party
or how it emerged, genie-like,
out of an abandoned shell case.
The weeds and their friends the shitting
pigeons want to bury this shrine
in a single summer.
I am holding the shovel for my father
while he reads inscriptions on brass:
sixteen golden names of the Party,
the twenty-six grammatical flaws.

NOVEMBER IN BOSTON
for Paul and Hualing

In this place an Irishman should feel at home.
Walking from the Shamrock Restaurant into the theatre
district I cross Lismore and Waterford streets,
abundant whiskey faces, even a tricolour shyly flown
in a pub window. The cool November air
is damp and gusty, pure Atlantic, unlike the neat

interior breezes that cross the Mid-West. The older
Irish have flown by now to the warm southern places
where the sun and accents are broad and unfamiliar.
Today, people without consonants brave the Boston air;
Asian and beautiful, they Zen-ify the open spaces
where white Sweeneys had fantasized on sex and beer.

One Sunday, from a studio I looked over disused wharves
at the little Ireland. "Snow comes down on our streets
like an extra drop of oil," the young artist said,
"blending Asian and Irish memory into its scarf
of white." As he spoke people fled from a hard sleet;
rich Bostonians and labourers with luncheons of bread.

Those long November evenings I was made to feel as special
as a kiwi, a small green species resurrected from
its island grave. "Listen! He's Irish! From back there."
It took an hour of words for expectations to dispel,
for them to find a space for one *Sweeney* gone all calm
and clean-cut, like a piece of superior export crystal.

THE DYING SYNAGOGUE
AT SOUTH TERRACE

Chocolate-coloured paint and the July sun
like a blow-torch peeling off
the last efforts of love.
More than time has abandoned this,
God's abandonment, God's synagogue,
that rose out of the ocean
one hundred years from here.
The peeling paint is an immigrant's
guide to America—lost on the shore
at Cobh, to be torn and scored

by a city of *luftmenshn*;
Catholics, equally poor, equally driven.

To have been through everything,
to have suffered everything and left
a peeling door. *Yahweh* is everywhere,
wherever abandonment is needed—
a crow rising after an accident,
wearing the grey uniform
of a bird of carrion, a badger
waiting for the bones of life
to crack before letting go:
wishing the tenth cantor to die,
the Synagogue to become a damp wall,
the wailing mouths to fester.
Too small. To be a small people
aligned to nothing is to suffer blame
like a thief in the night. An activist
threw a petrol-bomb for Palestine:

the sky opened and rained hail
like snow-drops. Flowers for memory,
petrol for the far-away.
To name one's land is to be a cuckoo
pushing others, bird-like, into a pit:
until, at the end, every sacred gesture
becomes vain, soiling the Synagogue
door like the charcoal corpses
at Mauthausen Station, 1944. A few
survived in the green valley of know-
nothing: spent themselves putting boots
on the Catholic poor, counting the brown
pennies, the corncrakes on their
trade routes, and the guerilla raids.

To sit here now, in the rancid sunshine
of low tide, is to contemplate

all of the unnoticed work of love—
exquisite children fall like jewels
from an exhausted colporteur's bag:
a mid-century daughter practises piano,
an *etude* to forget terror; a brother
dreams of the artistic life, another
shall practise law and become, in time,
the Catholic's tall Lord Mayor.
Where these jewels fall beside the peeling
door, let us place the six lilies of memory;
the six wounds of David's peeling star.

Aidan Carl Matthews

b. 1956

MINDING RUTH
for Seamus Deane

She wreaks such havoc in my library,
It will take ages to set it right—
A Visigoth in a pinafore

Who, weakening, plonks herself
On the works of Friedrich Nietzsche,
And pines for her mother.

She's been at it all morning,
Duck-arsed in my History section
Like a refugee among rubble,

Or, fled to the toilet, calling
In a panic that the seat is cold.
But now she relents under biscuits

To extemporise grace notes,
And sketch with a blue crayon
Arrow after arrow leading nowhere.

My small surprise of language,
I cherish you like an injury
And would swear by you at this moment

For your brisk chatter brings me
Chapter and verse, you restore
The city itself, novel and humming,

Which I enter as a civilian
Who plants his landscape with place-names.
They stand an instant, and fade.

Her hands sip at my cuff. She cranes,
Perturbedly, with a book held open
At plates from Warsaw in the last war.

Why is the man with the long beard
Eating his booboos? And I stare
At the old rabbi squatting in turds

Among happy soldiers who die laughing,
The young one clapping: you can see
A wedding band flash on his finger.

PERSONS UNKNOWN

I can manage so few of you.
That fourteenth century face,
Distant with attentiveness, is beyond me;
And your stumble, outraged, to the kitchen,
A mauled finch in each fist.

Nor have I come to grips
With the picked roses you plant again
In diagonal rain outside a verandah,
Or coped with your stopping traffic
For a duck stalking with her troop.

The parking ticket, a chipped flask
Left on a dead son's desk for months,
I can wrestle with; as also
Type-written notes at night on my pillow,
Signed in bold Roman with your full name.

Most, I must take to heart
Those diary entries that commemorate
Festivals of grievance in a locked room
Where—a slip shading the standard lamp—
The small hours find you speechless, writing.

That much I can mean with names,
The enormous spaces without room
To move in, that inhabit us both:
Integrities of migraine. So, tonight,
As you describe that tumour

Thickening like winestains on a tablecloth—
My brother draining toward silence—
I too can say nothing, can commit nothing
But must stoop through a curve of zero
To prop two turf-bars in a carved grate,

And listen to the blue sprigs blazing
Fiercely in ooze of yellow: jammed
Uprights that harden and thin
Like the locked wrists of arm wrestlers
Forced slowly to the tops of tables.

AT THE WAILING WALL
i.m. my brother John, 1945–1978

I make free with old albums,
Photographs that show
Your good side in profile.
From them all, I would choose
Shots of the Wailing Wall
Weeks after the truce
And the fall of Jerusalem.
Because I too stand

At the blank wall of a death
Not granted or forgiven—
Her pavilion sacked by louts,
Her scriptures shat upon—
I recall you by picturing
A skull-cap and prayer-shawl,
Arms bare to the wrist
And lifted in hosanna,
Like that print of the Baptist
Wading through Jordan.

Your head is bent forward
Toward a future unheard-of,
A four-year illness;
And the lightly downed neck
That I clung to on rides,
Burnt only by sunlight:
Neither hairless nor sutured.

Sean Dunne

b. 1956

REFUGEES AT COBH

We were sick of seeing the liners leave
   With our own day in, day out, so when
The boats came with refugees to Cobh
   It was worth the fare to travel
From Cork to glimpse them on railed decks.
   They seemed like ourselves, which became
Disappointing. Their clothes were different:
   Dark coats and scarves like shawls,
Shoes heavy as anvils. Their talk
   Thickened: accents the sounds of rocks
Crumbling and crunching in quarries. *Latvia,*
   A word to spill. We pushed pins
In the names of their towns and regions,
   A homeland rife with altered borders.
They hadn't a word of English but we gave
   What we could: sheets and rationed tea,
Sweets, blankets, bread, bottles of stout.
   One night they sang for hours and we
Heard their songs pour over the islands,
   Not one of us knowing the words.
That music stayed in the mind afterwards:
   I can still see the lights of Haulbowline
Shimmering as songs broke among waves
   And afterwards moonlight fell on silence,
A flotsam of quiet like a bombed shore.
   So strange to see emigrants to Ireland
Huddled near posters telling us to leave
   The broken farms for Manhattan streets.
It was our Ellis Island: hunched
   Lines of foreigners with bundles

Staring at the grey cathedral, the terraces
    Of houses curved like icing around
Hills where handkerchiefs fluttered.
    In time we turned them away. Most stood
Steady as cattle when the ship drew out
    With pilot boats trailing after it,
Kittens drawn after a mother cat.
    Without them, there was one thing less
To do, one reason less to stay and stare
    At the ocean choking on words for home.

THROWING THE BEADS

A mother at Shannon, waving to her young
Son setting out from North Kerry, flung
A rosary beads out to the tarmac
Suddenly as a lifebelt hurled from a pier.
Don't forget to say your prayers in Manhattan.
Dangling between ticket and visa,
She saw the bright crucifix among skyscrapers,
Shielding him from harm in streets out of serials,
Comforting as a fat Irish cop in a gangster film
Rattling his baton along a railing after dark.

Greg Delanty

b. 1958

TIE

Without asking, you borrowed your father's black tie
Sure that he had another black tie to wear
Should some acquaintance or relation die.
But had he? He should be here somewhere.
But where? Could he be at home on this dark day,
Ransacking drawer after drawer for a funeral tie?
Yes, that must be what has kept him away.
Though you are sure you saw him, tieless,
Smiling over at you, before you lost him again
Among the keening cortege. Leaving you clueless
To his whereabouts, till earth, splattering a coffin
(Or was it the wind ululating in each prayer?),
Informed you that you can never give your father
Back his black tie, though you'll find him everywhere.

THE GIFT

You seek refuge
    from bee-mad weather
        in your book-strewn room
& notice a picture
    of a lone figure
        trudging an endless,
snow-laden path
    bordered by birdless trees
        (one of her sometime gifts).

You can almost hear
     the wind blow
          through careening boughs
& sense
     the wayfarer's rage
          at the snow-smarting day;
for you have travelled
     in such a scene
          (ever since she went away).

THRUST & PARRY

You're sure you heard something break. Something snap.
Deep within her. Like a twig split in two
And cast in the fire. Or like the snap
Of a violin string, halting all music.
And witnessing tears break in her face
You discovered the magic, the black magic,
Of your words, no magic could take back.
And, loathing the terrifying maniac in you,
You shattered a vase of flowers and fled,
As if from yourself, out into the dark.
Leaving her to pick up the flowers,
Restring the violin, await your next attack,
But this time of fawning words & flowers,
And her breakfast in bed for at least a week.

Michael O'Loughlin

b. *1958*

CUCHULAINN

If I lived in this place for a thousand years
I could never construe you, Cuchulainn.
Your name is a fossil, a petrified tree
Your name means less than nothing.
Less than Librium, or Burton's Biscuits
Or Phoenix Audio-Visual Systems—
I have never heard it whispered
By the wind in the telegraph wires
Or seen it scrawled on the wall
At the back of the children's playground.

Your name means less than nothing
To the housewife adrift in the Shopping Centre
At eleven-fifteen on a Tuesday morning
With the wind blowing fragments of concrete
Into eyes already battered and bruised
By four tightening walls
In a flat in a tower-block
Named after an Irish Patriot
Who died with your name on his lips.
But watching TV the other night
I began to construe you, Cuchulainn;
You came on like some corny revenant
In a black-and-white made for TV
American Sci-Fi serial.
An obvious Martian in human disguise
You stomped about in big boots
With a face perpetually puzzled and strained
And your deep voice booms full of capital letters:
What Is This Thing You Earthlings Speak Of

192

Dermot Bolger

b. 1959

DUBLIN GIRL, MOUNTJOY, 1984
(do Nuala)

I dreamt it all, from end to end, the carriageway,
The rivulet behind the dairy streaked with crystal,
A steel moon glinting in a guttered stream of rain,
And the steep hill that I would crest to find her,
My child asleep in my old bedroom beside my sister.

I dreamt it all, and when I woke, furtive girls
Were clambering onto the bars of the windows,
White shapes waving against the sky's uniform,
Praying for hands to reply from the men's cells
Before screws broke up the vigil of handkerchiefs.

I dreamt it all, the times I swore, never again
To walk that carriageway, a rivulet of fear glowing
In my veins until I shivered within its aftertaste
And hid with my child in the closed down factory
Where my brain snapped like a brittle fingernail.

I dreamt it all, the longing to touch, the seance
In the cell when we screamed at the picture falling,
The warmth of circled hands after the numbing glass
Between my child and me, a warder following her words
To be rationed out and lived off for days afterwards.

I dreamt of you, who means all to me, my daughter,
How we might run to that carriageway by the rivulet,
And when I woke a blue pupil was patrolling my sleep,
Jailing my dreams into the empty orbit of its world
Narrowed down to a spyhole, a globed eyelid closing.

from THE STARDUST SEQUENCE

Last night in swirling colour we danced again
and as strobelights stunned in black and white
I reached in this agony of slow motion for you
but you danced on as if cold light still shone
merging into the crowd as my path was blocked
by snarling bouncers & the dead eyed club owner

When I screamed across the music nobody heard
I flailed under spotlights like a disco dancer
and they formed a circle clapping to the beat
as I shuddered round the club in a violent fit
hurling through a dream without trembling awake
I revolved through space until I hit the ground

Lying among their feet tramping out the tunes
I grasped you inside my mind for this moment
your white dress bobbing in a cool candleflame
illuminating the darkness spinning towards me
a teenage dancing queen proud of her footwork
sparks rising like stardust all over the floor

Alan Moore

b. 1960

GIRLS' SCHOOL

March beyond green outskirts:
clouds are blousy dawn-flirts. . . .

A long school scarf, the driveway
trails the feet of chestnut trees.
Behind oaks, radios seem to be being tuned.
Birds study their toes.
Down in the hockey field, the gardener
sits like a monkey on a mower
that exhales green exclamation marks,
his jacket limp on the lawn, a dead dog.

Chatter echoes in corridors. Coats conspire.
Every locker hoards its pair of milk-white sneakers.
Under cover of a desk, twin apples let go their scents.
Pencils throstle in a nest.
A hedgehog hairbrush peeps from a handbag.

In the gym, Hitler mädchen
sit crosslegged around flasks and sandwiches,
little Marilyns, winking their approval
of *Meatloaf* and *Adam and the Ants*,
the wispy titles that tattoo
their camouflaged satchels.

Outside, under crimped zinc,
dewy bicycles mount. Spokes glitter.
Whichever elm is examined, silver lacework trembles,
leaves sway in an Austrian wedding waltz,
leaf-light cascades like confetti.

With a torturer's tongs, his brogues clinching gravel,
the gardener snips carefully at a fringe
where snowdrops present themselves like debutantes.
He picks one gently, smiles like a Pope.

Peter Sirr

b. 1960

'PHONING

Your voice bleeds bafflement and anger
into my drowsiness. *Why such pointless waste?*
I search for the something there must always be to say
and remember the last time you were here,
sweet and girlish, as you probed
another sadness,
undressing my rage with your hands.
Saddened again, we dial the healing digits
and breathe a hug down the line
we'd saved for love
and open now to silence, the death of friends,
the crackle of the freakish and banal.

TROUBADOUR

For once it doesn't matter that you've gone.
I have retired to the quiet balcony
facing a hundred others, there are sheds and trees,
cats thrilling the meagre spaces
and for once I fail to imagine
those unfinished lessons, the yap of television
in your distant room. I have nothing to do
now, till the lights appear
in my neighbours' kitchens and I can smell
at least six different cuisines, but go on
opening and opening the small gift of your body,
holding to the tang, that winey, cunty herb
every breeze has shaken.

Katie Donovan

b. 1962

FIRST AUTUMN NIGHT
(for Martin)

In the first Autumn night
I open my window,
Looking for your flame
To roar into me
From beyond the moon's
Pearl-cool gaze;
My nostrils reach
For your smell
From the leaf-damp air,
Your white, flaring laugh
From the mottled rustlings
In the eaves,
But the night toad squats, unmoved,
His fat throat
Flickers dark green,
He has swallowed the sun,
His dank hide eclipses your face,
The trees sweep you away
With their weary arms
Like the last of summer;

I turn in
To my doll-yellow robe,
Where pieces of you dart
Unfinished and awry—
Your head a sunflower,
(Blue birds, your eyes),
Your firefingers on my skin,
The hot caprice of your tongue,

The eager blaze of your sex,
Your long thigh
Ember warm on mine—

I pull you around me
Like a golden skin,
Liked a patched blanket
In the first Autumn chill.

WE WERE SISTERS WEREN'T WE

I stifled in that room
On the edge of that double bed
You in your red cotton gown
Hugging the other edge.
Backs to each other
I could feel your burnished hair
Warning me off, sparking on the pillow!
Keep to your side.
Not that I was anxious to flail about
My pudgy toes accidentally nudge
Your cold huddled feet.
I was hot, I ripped off my choking
Flowered flanellette gown,
Pushed into my hand by our hostess, fussing.
It hissed to the ground and
I moved carefully, letting my flesh spread.
You were so far away
Yet I scarcely dared to turn over—
You might decide to turn at the same time.
Then we would have to feign sleep face to face.
Because neither of us slept.
I sighed and rustled, so did you, but
It was too intimate for the
Feints of words.

I itched and wriggled
Raw in my skin in that hot bed
Nervous of your red sprite body
So slimly, ethereally there,
Restless too, but not naked, not sweating.
I had thought nothing of our sharing
This bed, we were like sisters weren't we
But I couldn't relax.
Barbed sisterhood, territorially alert
Anxious to avoid collision.
In the morning, gravel-eyed,
I heard your polite yawn
Quick night-gown held hop out of bed
To the solitary relief of a hot bath.

Sara Berkeley

b. 1967

LEARNING TO COUNT

Sounds in the dim washed room
Like the sound in a mother's throat as she takes her baby
    back
The music of blossom, and sight
From the stars always yellow over where she lies
In one, fine, expansive gesture of sleep.
The child whose hand I couldn't let go
Even when we found sticks and things with wings.
We threw them and they flew.

She learns at last to be silent and be still
And I no longer follow where she sleeps, running through the
    dreams
That came so fast—dreams like white metal
Bright up from the fire. In one we ran so far
Past wet ground with the wet brown trees leaning on us
So dripping grey and I thought   She should be at school.
But the best bit, the most frightening,
Was after all the running when the wet lanes were past—
An angular house with the walls marching round us
And a woman at the door. Her apron was the only white
    thing
Like on canvas the afternoon dripped brown and grey,
Even though that woman had roses above her door.

It is falling cold outside.
I think of women who have roses above their doors.
And weep into their aprons.
Those are the ones with sons who always died in the war

The photographs burning into firelit sideboards
While up from the flames they come—as young sons do.

Over there, she sleeps through the shrouded night
She blooms with such pretty grace, snapping in my hand
Like the daffodil, dusting my fingers with the dry powder of
    her lust
Curving from the earth as she will,
Neither drooping nor withered. But now she sings nothing at
    all
But the shy, resilient beat of the nursery rhymes from school.

Index of Poets and Translators

Index of First Lines of Poems

Acknowledgments

Permission to use copyright material is gratefully acknowledged to the following:
Anvil Press and the authors for poems by Thomas Mc Carthy and Alan Moore. Arlen Press and Carcanet and the author for poems by Eavan Boland. Beaver Row and Bloodaxe and the author for poems by Brendan Kennelly. Blackstaff Press and the author for poems by Paul Durcan and the estate of John Hewitt. Commons Press and the author for poems by Gerry Murphy. Dedalus Press and the author for a poem by John F. Deane. Dolmen Press and the author for poems by Greg Delanty. Faber and Faber (Boston) and the author for poems by Tom Paulin. Farrar, Straus & Giroux and the author for poems by Seamus Heaney. Gallery Press and the authors for poems by Ciarán Carson, Harry Clifton, Gerald Dawe, Seamus Deane, Peter Fallon, Aidan Carl Matthews, James Simmons, Peter Sirr. Goldsmith Press, Douglas Sealy and Tomás MacSiomóin for translations of Maírtín Ó Direain in *Tocar Dánta/ Selected Poems*. Menard Press and the author for poems by Brian Coffey. Northpoint Press and the author for poems by Eamon Grennan. Raven Arts and the authors for poems by Sara Berkeley, Dermot Bolger, Philip Casey, Katie Donovan, Michael O'Loughlin, Francis Stuart; the author and Paul Muldoon for two translations of Michael Davitt; the author, John Montague, Paul Muldoon, and Michael Longley for translations of Nuala Ní Dhomhnaill in *Tonn Gael*; the author and Gabriel Fitzmaurice for translations of Michael Hartnett in *Tonn Gael*. Secker and Warburg and the author for poems by Matthew Sweeney. Wake Forest University Press and the authors for poems by Thomas Kinsella, Michael Longley, Derek Mahon, Medbh MacGuckian, John Montague, Paul Muldoon, Richard Murphy. The poets Sean Dunne, Patrick Galvin, James Liddy, Desmond O'Grady for their works.
In some cases it has not been possible to establish the exact provenance of American or world rights, and we apologize in advance for any omission.

JOHN MONTAGUE is the author of eight collections of poetry and the editor of Macmillan's *Book of Irish Verse* (1974), which was called "a fine broth of a book" by *Saturday Review* and an "indispensable guide" by *The New York Times Book Review*. Born in Brooklyn, New York, he moved to Ireland at the age of four and was brought up on a farm in Ulster. He was educated at University College, Dublin, and Yale University, and was professor of English at the University of Cork from 1972 to 1988, when he retired to become a full-time writer again. Montague was writer-in-residence with the New York State Writers Institute in 1985, the first to be sponsored by the Institute, and is the first to hold the title of Distinguished Professor there.